You can become whole again

You can become *whole* again

A Guide to Healing for
the Christian in Grief

Jolonda Miller

 John Knox Press
ATLANTA

Library of Congress Cataloging in Publication Data

Miller, Jolonda, 1945–
  You can become whole again.

  Bibliography: p.
  1. Bereavement. 2. Grief. 3. Consolation.
I. Title
BV4905.2.M53   248.8′6   80–84652
ISBN 0–8042–1156–6   AACR2

© copyright 1981 John Knox Press
10 9 8 7 6 5 4 3 2 1
Printed in the United States of America
John Knox Press
Atlanta, Georgia 30365

All mankind is of one Author,
and is one volume; when one Man dies,
one Chapter is not torn out of the book,
but translated into a better language,
and every Chapter must be so translated.

John Donne, *Devotions*, XVII

to Sherrill

acknowledgements

No book as intensely personal as this one easily writes itself. Rather, it requires the support and help of special people as well as the writer's own desire and ability for putting his or her experience to good use. In addition to the faithful and able leadership of God's Spirit, I've been blessed with the encouragement and assistance of people whom I wish to acknowledge here:

Helen Bass, the first Christian to minister to my grief in the Lord's love, and who has given unflaggingly of her prayers, emotional support, and practical assistance in the writing of the manuscript. Without her interest and confidence in this book, I doubt it would have been written.

Peggy Futch, my confidante and sister-in-Christ, who has been the kind of Christian friend I describe in this book. Primarily through her capacity for caring and loyalty in friendship, the Lord has helped me to learn constructive grief and has made me whole again. Without the experiences I've had in sharing with Peggy, and she with me, there would have been no book to write.

Rob and Debbie Miller, two very special children, who have done their best to support me with their love for me, their confidence in me, and their cooperation with me while "Mommy writes on her book."

And I also wish to recognize the countless other friends and relatives who have consistently prayed for me in my grief and in the building of a new life. Their comfort, assistance, and understanding can never be adequately expressed in terms of what those things have meant to me.

contents

for the reader

July 6, 1973. The following day would be a special one, the eighth anniversary of my marriage to Sherrill Miller. It had been a good, stable marriage. We had survived a year of separation while he served in Vietnam. We'd gone through a change in lifestyle and career when we left Army life for civilian life. And we had started a family, with a son born in 1970 and a daughter who was not yet four months old. "A boy to replace me and now a girl to replace you," Sherrill had proudly told me a few hours after her birth. Everything was going great. Life was good to us, and we expected it to get even better as the years rolled by.

But the years of togetherness were drawing to a close. By evening of that July day, a boating accident would leave me a widow and our two young children fatherless.

I was in the boat with my husband when it happened. By the grace of God and Sherrill's efforts to save me from drowning, I am alive today. In the ensuing months of deep grief and the struggle to start a new life without him, I often wondered why God chose to take his life but not my own. Purpose in living became more important to me than ever before. Perhaps this book is part of that purpose.

Every word I have written in the body of this book comes from my heart. I have known that kind of utter desolation and overwhelming emotional pain you may be suffering from in your loss. I have experienced many of the grief problems I describe herein. I know what it's like to feel some of the things you may be feeling.

Also, what I write comes from my head. I have learned how to grieve constructively, and I believe that you, too, with the help of God, can become whole again. If what I write out of my understanding of the experience is of the smallest help to one reader alone, I shall be most thankful.

And last, but surely not the least of these, every word comes to you through the love of Jesus Christ. Without doubt, I know him to be the God of all comfort and healing. I earnestly believe that he wants to guide you into wholeness because he has done the same for me.

My suggestion is that you read these selections at the pace most comfortable for you. You may want to read one a day. Their brevity allows them to fit in with the busiest of schedules. Or you may want to read along until you feel the need to stop. Some of what I say to you may be so direct and abrupt that you can only take it a little at a time. If that should be the case, please bear in mind that I write to you with the deepest kind of love and understanding. If I seem "tough" on you at certain points, it's because I know that people who are coddled in their grief are not likely to let it heal and grow from it.

At the end of this volume is a list of suggestions for further reading. These are highly valuable resources which I have found helpful in my own grief work. It is by no means a comprehensive list; however, most of the books contain bibliographies of their own which can acquaint you with even more resources. My reason for including such a list is that this little book is quite basic and elementary. Should these selections raise any questions in your mind about what I've written or neglected to say, the books in this list may serve to answer them.

Now, as you begin to read, please know that I am with you in prayerful thought. May the grace and peace of our Lord Jesus Christ, who gives us our kinship in him, be with your spirit as you read. And may you be led by the power of his Spirit into wholeness of life again.

—Jolonda Miller

Take care
of your grief

"These things just happen," some may sadly shake their heads and say.

"It was God's will," others add.

And all the while your mind may be screaming a silent reply, "But it hurts! All I know is that it hurts!"

Forget the clichés of condolences. Forget their suggestions of defeat and do-nothingness. You need to know what's going on inside you. You need to understand what has happened and the effects it's having on your whole being. Why? So that you can know what you're dealing with, learn how to cope with it, and eventually recover from it.

Suppose in one month's time you receive a promotion, get transferred to another city, and purchase your first home. And after a few months, you realize you aren't staying within your budget. If you say to yourself, "Well, these things happen," and do nothing to investigate your spending and try to correct the situation, you may soon find yourself in deep financial trouble.

Or suppose a well-established, valuable friendship suddenly cools and remains that way for weeks. You have no idea as to why, but your friend is distant, reserved, and not as accessible to you as before. If you think, "This must be God's will for us," and do nothing to find out what's gone wrong in the relationship, you may needlessly lose your friend altogether.

But you probably would not have failed to act in such matters. When trouble threatens or becomes evident in the necessary and valuable parts of your life, your first impulse, most likely, would be to determine what's happening. Second, to remedy the things within the situation that can be taken care of. Third, to adjust to the things you cannot change for the moment. And last, to set new goals for improvement in the future.

But when death occurs, leaving you in the shock wave of emotional upheaval, you may not be so conscientious in taking care of the most necessary and valuable thing you have, your self. That's because sometimes the emotional pain of losing overtakes the natural impulses to investigate, understand, implement, adapt, and set new goals for the rest of life. But it doesn't have to stay that way for you. Indeed, for your own spiritual, emotional, and physical welfare, you must not allow it to permanently immobilize you.

Forget all the expectations others have for your grief. Establish some of your own. Realistic expectations you know you can meet. Then proceed one step at a time in understanding and dealing with your grief.

The ways in which death of another can turn your life inside out and upside down are very real and painful, I know. But such a tragedy doesn't have to be a permanent obstacle to your responsibility and privilege to really live the rest of your life. Don't let it be so for you.

Psalm 61:1–2
> Hear my cry, O God;
>> listen to my prayer.
> From the ends of the earth I call to you,
>> I call as my heart grows faint;
>> lead me to the rock that is higher than I.

Matthew 11:28–29
> "Come to me, all you who are weary and burdened, and I will give you rest. Take my yoke upon you and learn from me, for I am gentle and humble in heart, and you will find rest for your souls."

Dear Father, how glad I am that I can call you Father and expect that you will hear me and come to me just as surely as a loving parent goes to a child who cries out in the night. I am like that child, Lord. I feel such searing, painful anguish deep inside me. I feel so confused at what has happened. Nothing's clear or sane to me any more. Everything has fallen apart. I don't know what to do, Lord! Except to turn to you. In Jesus' name, please help me. Amen.

2

Understand
your crisis

Don't let yourself get lost in your crisis. Understand what has happened to you and how it is affecting you right now. Think in terms of past, present, and future.

The past action that has brought you to where you are is death. Someone you loved, perhaps depended upon and needed, is dead. That person died, and is gone from this life, not to return. You had no control over it then; you have no control over it now, for it is past, finished, over. And you must accept it. You may never have allowed yourself to think about the possibility of that death, or you may have dreaded it at the most. But it happened, and you must internalize that fact by accepting it in your head and in your heart.

When death takes away, it leaves a wound. Presently, you are suffering from that wound. It's a natural consequence. Because we do not want the ones we love to die, it's only natural that we grieve when they do. And grief can affect your outward life as well as your inward feelings. Perhaps you find it hard to be interested in your work or taking care of your family and household. Perhaps you are no longer able to think straight when it comes to decision-making. Perhaps you actually feel physical manifestations of your inner pain. The onslaught of grief can do these things to you. Be aware that they can. Start preparing yourself intellectually to meet them.

When you're physically injured, you see the future as a time for healing. Allow the same necessity for an emotional wound. Don't say to yourself that you can't go on living without the one you've lost. Tell yourself, "I must go on, and I can!" Keep ever in mind that the rest of your life awaits you. You've got some living yet to do. Make the most of it.

Isaiah 40:31
> But those who hope in the LORD
>   will renew their strength.
> They will soar on wings like eagles;
>   they will run and not grow weary,
>   they will walk and not be faint.

John 14:27
> "Peace I leave with you; my peace I give to you. I do not give to you as the world gives. Do not let your hearts be troubled and do not be afraid."

John 16:33
> "In this world you will have trouble. But take heart! I have overcome the world."

O Lord, if only I could see right now that I can go on and will make it through this. This pit of sorrow seems so wide and so deep that I wonder if it has any walls or bottom! I feel encompassed by my grief. How can I possibly "take heart"? But you knew such grief, too, didn't you, Father? You know how I feel, for you allowed your own dear Son to suffer and die a horrible, humiliating death for the likes of me. And he is my only hope now because victory is in him. Will you lead me to the peace he gives? Will you comfort me as no one else can? In Christ's name. Amen.

Take care of your body

Losing someone you love affects your entire being. Grief is felt physically, emotionally, and spiritually. Quite often a person in grief dwells on the emotions and spirit but neglects the body. The inner pain is of such a magnitude and the spiritual questions are so profound and demanding that the need to physically survive is overshadowed by them. You forget to eat, or you don't eat well. You drive yourself hard and forget to rest. You don't sleep well, or you sleep too little.

All of this is quite understandable. But the fact remains that your physical health is just as important now as it has ever been—even more so if your loss has added new areas of responsibility to the ones you already bear.

So, first things first. Are you taking good care of your body? Have you had a physical checkup in the last year or so? Are you ignoring the body's signals that are trying to tell you something somewhere needs attention?

Don't put the proverbial cart before the horse. Your body is the only vehicle you have for living this life effectively. You can deal far better with the emotional pain and the spiritual seeking if physically you are feeling as well as possible.

Remember that you are a tripartite being of spirit, soul, and body. When one part suffers neglect, it can bring the others down with it. Take care of every part of you.

1 Corinthians 6:19

> Do you not know that your body is a temple of the Holy Spirit, who is in you, whom you have received from God?

2 Samuel 12:20–23

> . . . After [David] had washed, put on lotions and changed his clothes, he went into the house of the LORD and worshiped. Then . . . he ate.
>
> His servants asked him, "Why are you acting this way? While the child was alive, you fasted and wept, but now that the child is dead, you get up and eat!"
>
> He answered, "While the child was still alive, I fasted and wept. . . . But now that he is dead, why should I fast? Can I bring him back again? I will go to him, but he will not return to me."

Dear God, this pain that holds me has befuddled my thinking. I neglect my physical self without even realizing it. I forget too easily that you have made your home in my body. Thank you for reminding me. Help me to remember to take good care of myself. Keep me physically well so that I can better meet the challenge of this grief. In your name. Amen.

Get your head together

Emotional anguish and suffering can be debilitating. You don't think of doing logical, rational things because your pain is so intense. But you must make the effort. You must take care of your physical self and at the same time begin to get your head together.

If you face a major decision, such as moving or changing jobs, delay it if possible until you can think it through. If it can't be postponed and you find your thinking is confused, seek the counsel of others you know who can give sound advice. Weigh their suggestions carefully, and then decide for yourself in terms of what *you* want for your life. Avoid the impulse to act too quickly in order to "get it over with." Remember, you are in the midst of a life-changing crisis, and you may not make a wise decision if you act too hastily. Slow down. Take things as they come. Give yourself time to get yourself together.

And practice saying goodbye. The cause of your crisis is the departure of your loved one. To get yourself together and go on from here, you've got to learn to say goodbye.

Exercise that mental hold within you that clings to the one you love until it becomes pliable enough to let go. An emotional and mental letting go does not mean, "I don't love you any more," or "I am deserting you and forgetting all you ever meant to me." Rather, it's a response to the other's farewell that's already been said. The one you've lost has left this life; you've got to respond to his final goodbye.

This kind of final acceptance of your loved one's death won't come automatically with the first goodbye. You may have to release him to death and to the Lord again and again before your heart assents to what you intellectually know to be true. So, practice saying good-bye. And one day you'll be able to say, "I release you from the living. I mentally and emotionally allow you to depart from this life to where you are now."

Isaiah 41:10
> "So do not fear, for I am with you;
>   do not be dismayed, for I am your God.
> I will strengthen you and help you;
>   I will uphold you with my righteous right
>   hand."

2 Corinthians 12:9
> But he said to me, "My grace is sufficient for
> you, for my power is made perfect in weak-
> ness."

Lord, I just want to get away from all this. I don't want to make any decisions. I don't want to practice saying goodbye. I don't want to do the things I know I must do. But I have to, don't I? I have to face the realities left in the wake of this loss like so much driftwood brought to shore by a stormy sea. A stormy sea—I've been in the midst of it, and I haven't recovered my equilibrium yet. Still, the beach needs caretaking, or it will become an eyesore of pollution heaped upon pollution. So, once again, I acknowledge my dependence on you. Hold me up with your strong, victorious hand, and help me to do what I must do. In Jesus' name. Amen.

Attend to your spirit

Pay attention to your spirit as well as to your outward and inner selves. Remember that your whole person is affected by your loss. Take care of your most inward self, too.

Now is the time for leaning on those ever-lasting arms of God. They are strong and able to carry all the grief of this world. Let them wrap around your spirit, and you will experience with your emotions the love, peace, and understanding that are there.

Come near to God through prayer, reading his Word, and meditating upon who he is and all his good and wonderful qualities. Come to him as his child, and open yourself to his response to you as the loving, comforting Father he truly is.

Know that he is there, waiting for you to seek him. Let him strengthen your inner person and give power to your faith. Let him, by asking him to do these things, expecting he will do them, and cooperating with him as he starts to move in your life.

Let your spirit seek comfort from the Source who gave it. But also, let it ask its questions. Feed it with the life-giving Word of God, the continuing two-way communication of prayer, and the spiritual guidance and encouragement available from your brothers- and sisters-in-Christ.

Psalm 34:18–19

>The LORD is close to the brokenhearted
>   and saves those who are crushed in spirit.
>A righteous man may have many troubles,
>   but the LORD delivers him from them all.

Jeremiah 29:13

>"You will seek me and find me when you
>seek me with all your heart."

O gracious Lord! How wonderful you are! Only by your infinite loving-kindness can you offer such good things to me. And only by my submission to you as my God can I receive them. Lord, help me to reach out to you as you reach out to me so that our hands may touch and you can lift me up to a safer, higher ground. Be with my spirit, Father. Embrace me with your everlasting arms, and let me feel their strength and love. In your strong and holy name I pray. Amen.

6

Get on with
the living

Life goes on the same as it always has. The
laundry must be done, meals must be prepared
for the family, a paycheck must be earned so that
the bills can be paid. The week still has seven
days, each with its own duties to be performed.
And the sun still rises every morning, bidding
you get out of bed and on with the day's activities.

For a brief while it seemed as if the whole
world had ended. But it didn't. For a time it
seemed as if your life had stopped. But, of
course, it didn't. You are a "survivor," the word
others use to label the bereaved. The question
is, what kind of survivor are you?

Do you go through all the outward motions
of life in robot-fashion? Or, are you one of those
who finds a "salvation" from grief in putting all
your psychic and physical energies into one outward area of your life, such as your job or your
children? Perhaps you're neither of these but
one who thinks a crutch, like alcohol or pills, is
necessary to survive.

None of these is living. You deserve a better
life than that.

True, once you've been dealt a heavy blow,
it takes time and extreme effort to get up again.
But when the initial shock begins to subside and

you're able to get up and start to move about, then is the time to get on with the living.

John 10:10
> "I have come that they may have life, and have it to the full."

Romans 8:28
> And we know that in all things God works for the good of those who love him, who have been called according to his purpose.

Dear Lord, it's hard enough just to survive. How can I also really live? How can my life become full when it is so empty? How can any good come from tragedy and heartache? Oh, I know I've seen it work for others or have heard of it. But those were other people, Lord, not me! Still, I can't deny that you have promised life to the full and good in all things to one such as I. Therefore, they must be possible, for you do not lie, you are faithful. Just help me, please, not to miss out on anything you want to bless me with. For I need your blessings, Lord. I need them so much! In Jesus' name. Amen.

Decide what you want to do

There is much more you can do with grief than just survive it. Being able to "take it" and endure life in spite of your loss may seem the brave thing to do, or even the *only* choice you have when tragedy comes.

But these two assumptions are wrong. Unhealthy, too. Such stoical endurance is in reality false courage. It takes no courage to avoid dealing with the unpleasant things that happen in life. Any coward can do that. But it does require the highest kind of courage to continue experiencing life, whatever the circumstance, and that's the other choice you have.

Which do you opt for? The alternative that seems the easiest—carrying on *in spite of* your loss? Or the one that seems most difficult but is in fact the most profitable in the long run—growing as a person *because of* your loss?

Only you can decide. Only you can want to stagnate in sorrow or grow, as you heal, in understanding more about life and death through grief. Don't say the choice depends upon what you can or cannot do. It's not a matter of "can" or "can't" but one of "will" or "won't."

That lays the responsibility for how you fare solely on your shoulders, doesn't it? Accept the fact, my friend, for that's exactly where responsibility for your recovery rests.

Romans 5:3–5

> Not only so, but we also rejoice in our sufferings, because we know that suffering produces perseverence; perseverance, character; and character, hope. And hope does not disappoint us, because God has poured out his love into our hearts by the Holy Spirit, whom he has given us.

Ezra 10:4

> "Rise up; this matter is in your hands. We will support you, so take courage and do it."

You won't let me off easy, will you, Lord? Self-pity feels so safe and secure, and here you are saying I must get out of the little shell I've created and make one of two choices. I thought I had no choice! But evidently I do. I don't understand it, however. I don't understand all this about healing and growing. Are they really possible for me? Will you really do more than just help me through the first few weeks of sorrow? Somehow I think you will, if I will let you. As much as I can be right now, I'm willing, Lord, to want what you want, for however long it takes for me to heal and grow. In the power of your Son's name. Amen.

8

Consider the choice you are making

You can become a whole person again. Recovery . . . renewal . . . wholeness—they may not seem probable outcomes of all you suffer right now, but they are possible. Possible even for you.

Others have suffered as much or more than what you're going through today. And many of them have experienced healing of their grief or are in the process of becoming whole again. Take a look around the next time you're in a bookstore. Their stories are there by the dozens.

And if it's happened for them, it can happen for you, can't it? You really are no exception to the rule. Nor can you claim not to "know how," especially since I'm about to reveal the secret of their success—they wanted to become whole again, and they were willing to work toward that goal.

Desire and willingness. They are prerequisites to the healing process the experts call "grief work." And that's an appropriate term. A task that often grows wearisome and long, it is indeed work. But it's also an investment that reaps the kind of benefits you just can't put a price tag on, because grief work is the way to wholeness, you see.

Consider what you want for yourself in the

rest of your life. Then think of where you're placing your investment now—in the ulcer or heart attack or nervous breakdown of tomorrow? Or in the kind of healing that makes you whole again?

Jeremiah 10:23
> I know, O LORD, that a man's life is not his own; it is not for man to direct his steps.

Isaiah 30:21
> Whether you turn to the right or to the left, your ears will hear a voice behind you, saying, "This is the way; walk in it."

I don't know about this "grief work" business, Lord. It sounds so cold and impersonal. Is it just a hollow sociological or psychological term, or is it a viable, practical alternative? Even though I have some doubts about it, it certainly sounds more attractive to me than those other "investments." If this "grief work" is what you want for me, Lord, then enhance my desire so that I can be more willing to face the task. If you want me on that road, please direct me there. In Jesus' blessed name. Amen.

9

Choose to become whole again

"Grief work." What does it mean? Isn't it just another funereal term like bereavement and sorrow? No, not quite. "Grief work" is not associated with death but with living.

Bereavement is a word used to define the circumstance of having been deprived of something or someone dear to you. It is the situation in which you now find yourself, the state of having recently lost a loved one.

Sorrow is a single word used to encompass all the various grief-feelings that result from having lost. It is the pain you are feeling.

In other words, bereavement is the outer circumstance that has happened to you. Sorrow is the inner state of feelings bereavement has left you in.

Now, bereavement is a fact. Nothing can ever reverse it. You can't do a thing about bringing your loved one back to you in this life. Nor can you find someone else to "be" that person for you. Accept that right now if you haven't already.

But you can do something about sorrow, something far better and healthier than wallowing in it or disowning all its feelings and putting on a brave front. You can work through your grief.

Listen to that phrase again: work *through* grief. It implies a process, doesn't it? And process means a beginning, a middle, and an end. In all honesty, I assure you that if you are willing to work through your grief, there is an end to sorrow awaiting you. Not an end to loving that person. Not an end to cherishing his memory. But an end to being in the grip of sorrow's pain.

Wouldn't you like to overcome your pain? Of course you would! You have a right not to hurt any more. You have more to do with the rest of your life than to be in a continuing state of sorrow for this one loss.

As with any other process, healing requires that you proceed from point A through point Y in order to get to point Z. And grief work is your means of getting there.

Psalm 37:5
> Commit your way to the LORD;
> trust in him and he will do this.

Isaiah 60:20
> The LORD will be your everlasting light,
> and your days of sorrow will end.

I see it more clearly now, Lord. I do want to become whole again. I understand now that I can do this—that is, you and I together can do this—by going through it instead of staying in it. You've allowed this dark tunnel to be placed squarely in the path of my life. There's no going around it, Lord, though I've wanted to. And it only hurts me more to sit near the entrance looking longingly at the past with a backward gaze. No, I must go through the tunnel. And with your gracious help and support, I'll see the light at the end of the tunnel someday. Just stay with me, please, for I'm awfully afraid of what may lie ahead in the dark. I ask in Christ's name. Amen.

Choose your companions in grief work

Grief is a lonely word. Even though many others may be grieving also for the loss of this one person, each of you is alone in grief. With one death, for instance, a mother loses a daughter; a husband, a wife; a child, a mother; a brother, a sister. The list can go on and on. The point is, each loss is individual and to itself because each relationship is different. It's even so in the case of friends; each friend's loss of the same friend is different. Thus, every instance of grief-reaction to the death of one person differs from all others, and each person is alone in his own particular grief.

Likewise, grief work is a lonely experience. Only you can do the grief work set before you. No one else can do it for you. But someone can go with you. Walk beside you. As a comfort, a support, a friend.

You need someone like that. Don't try to do it alone. Let someone else walk with you. Your strength is taxed as it is; don't think you can be martyr-like and succeed all by yourself.

But who is there to help? Who would even want to? You have three areas of resources. Tap them, and you'll discover your companions.

First and foremost, take the Lord with you. Don't leave him on the fringes; make him part of your inner circle. Be honest with him. Tell him exactly how it is, even when what you think or feel is contrary to what you know a Christian *should* think or feel. Get in touch with him through his Word and by listening to the voice of his Spirit. And make your requests known to him, expecting answers that will be for your benefit, for that's what he wants for you: your benefit. He wants your suffering to be alleviated; he wants your wound to heal; he wants you whole again, because he loves you and wants you to have a new, re-directed life.

And your second most important resource is yourself. Many times no one can help us much because we continue to defeat ourselves. So, be kind to yourself. Help yourself. Treat yourself as you would a beloved friend undergoing the same kind of suffering. And why shouldn't you? You are more than your suffering. You are a person, a child of the King. You deserve to become whole again. You have potential for growth you aren't even aware of. You can become a more mature person and Christian *because of* what has happened to you.

And third, ask the Lord to show you at least one trustworthy friend. It may be you already have that friend or will meet him soon. The Lord will supply; he knows you need someone to talk to, someone who wants to listen, to help, to see you become whole again. Someone who loves you and him. Someone whose life isn't wrapped up completely in yours or in your grief.

See? You are not really alone, though the task is solely yours. Take the hand of those reaching out to you. After all, isn't that what Christianity is all about?

Revelation 3:20
> "Here I am! I stand at the door and knock. If anyone hears my voice and opens the door, I will go in and eat with him, and he with me."

Matthew 18:20
> "For where two or three come together in my name, there am I with them."

Dear Lord, thank you so much that you care enough for me not to want me to be alone in this. Help me to be more closely and more frequently in touch with you day and night. Help me to be a good friend to myself. And help me, if you will, Lord, by sending me that special kind of friend I need. Help me to be open to your ministry to my needs in whatever forms you choose to send it. I praise you, Lord, and thank you for your interest in my life and your desire to meet my every need. These things I ask for in the strong name of Jesus Christ. Amen.

Take the Lord with you

Put Christ in the center of your grief. If you want his kind of peace comforting your mind, his kind of love embracing your heart, his kind of wisdom guiding your decisions, and his kind of power strengthening you and enabling your task of going forward from here.

Remember that his Spirit is alive, energetic, and moving in today's world. He is available to you to appropriate within your life all his qualities, gifts, and fruitfulness. And he wants so much to do this. He wants to fill your whole life as well as indwell you.

Don't settle for a half-full cup, or even a full one. Desire the cup continually running over, spilling all over your life and touching the lives of others.

The apostles wrote that we suffer because we must share in Christ's sufferings if we are to share in his inheritance also. They wrote that our sufferings serve to refine us into gold. And that God wants to comfort us in our sufferings so that we in turn may be able to give comfort to others. These things can come about only if we cooperate with the Holy Spirit, letting him fill us, letting him work in us, letting him change the parts of our selves that need changing.

So, when you visualize in your mind's eye the heartache you're going through, picture the Lord Jesus Christ and all his power as standing in the center of it all, feeling what you feel, and holding in his

hands all the good he wants to bring out of your circumstances. Keep him there and let him do those
wonders in your life.

Romans 8:31–32

> If God is for us, who can be against us? He who
> did not spare his own Son, but gave him up for
> us all—how will he not also, along with him, gra-
> ciously give us all things?

Philippians 4:13

> I can do everything through him who gives me
> strength.

*O Lord! How like you to not only want to do things for me
but also in and through me! Fill my cup, Lord, with the
presence of your good and powerful Spirit. Help me to learn
what you want me to learn through my suffering. Plant in
my mind the image of you and all your wonderful strength
and goodness as being in the midst of my sorrow. And bring
that picture to my remembrance each time I start to doubt
and despair. Thank you, Lord, that you really are in me,
and that Christ-in-me is much more than just a pretty
phrase or a theological thought. Help me to do what you
want me to do in the power of your Spirit within. In your
wonderful and holy name. Amen.*

Take a Christian friend with you

There's a difference between depending upon someone in time of need and being a burden. You know the difference. So don't let your pride or any false guilt for depending upon someone prevent you from accepting the friend you need in a time like this. You'll only deprive yourself of something special in the Christian life, as well as the Lord's provision for your genuine need.

Jesus knew of the human need to help and to be helped. He understood the value of involving other people in his ministry. Perhaps that's why he left the task of unbinding the grave clothes of Lazarus, whom he had just called forth from the dead, to the man's loved ones and neighbors standing about. He could have done it himself with a mere word or gesture of hand. You would think he would have wanted to, for Lazarus was a dear, personal friend of the Lord. But he didn't. Have you ever wondered why? Could it have been that he wanted the others he loved to share in the joy, as well as the responsibility, of his ministry? So that they could receive in giving as well as grow in faith?

Let the fellow Christian reaching out to you be your friend. Perhaps God has answered your prayer for help by sending this person as an instrument of his love and care.

Galatians 6:2

> Carry each other's burdens, and in this way you will fulfill the law of Christ.

1 Thessalonians 5:11

> Therefore encourage one another and build each other up.

Lord, I confess that even though I've prayed for this kind of friend, I may have thwarted you with my insistence on being "strong" and in no need of help when others have offered it. Why is it I do that? Yes, part of it is my pride. Perhaps even fear. And there are some people, Lord, I just don't want to minister to me. Their way of ministering doesn't suit my needs or even sometimes my personality. But surely there is someone you want to help me, whether it's a person who has already reached out to me or one who will. The truth is, I do need a friend, and you know exactly who will fit that need. So bring that person to me, Father, and help me to know it when you do. In Christ's name. Amen.

13

Accept your pain

The ironic thing about grief work is that those of us who are courageous enough to take on the task are usually unprepared for it. Very little in life educates us on how to grieve effectively and constructively. The older generation, who gave us our training in how to live, grieved for the most part in silence. Public schools may have taught us how to prepare a nutritious meal or how to change the spark plugs on a car, but little has been taught us regarding how to go about constructive grief.

How on earth does one go about grief work, then? There are no set rules or procedures. But there are some basic guidelines you can use to recognize your own particular needs and establish your own pace.

I have already mentioned that a person must want to heal and be willing to help himself to heal. Those having been established, the next question is, are you allowing yourself to feel the pain?

The hard truth that has to be faced here is that losing hurts. You are hurting. If you are being honest with yourself, you are consciously aware of that fact. Sometimes, however, pain is so hard to face that we push it below the surface of our conscious awareness. Even worse, we may put our feelings in the cellar of our minds until it is so far removed from our consciousness that we are no longer aware that it exists and is causing us problems. Either way, it's still there, bothering us, nagging at us like a thorn embedded in the flesh. Don't let this impulse to ignore your pain or psychologically deny it get a head start on you. Working through grief will be much harder if you do.

Instead, acknowledge your pain for what it is. Say it aloud to yourself, or to God, or to someone close to you. You see, acknowledgement of a feeling comes quickest when you verbalize it to someone else. In voicing a feeling, you are admitting it, confessing it, owning it. Only then can you deal with the pain itself. How many people do you know who are inclined to take good care of business they refuse to claim as their own? Probably none. You've got to say "this is pain and it is mine to take care of" before you'll ever be motivated toward healing.

John 11:33–35
> When Jesus saw her weeping, and the Jews who had come along with her also weeping, he was deeply moved in spirit and troubled. "Where have you laid him?" he asked.
> "Come and see, Lord," they replied.
> Jesus wept.

Matthew 26:37–38
> He took Peter and the two sons of Zebedee along with him, and he began to be sorrowful and troubled. Then he said to them, "My soul is overwhelmed with sorrow to the point of death. Stay here and keep watch with me."

O my dear sweet Lord! You knew such deep sorrow and pain. And you told your good friends; you owned it before them. But Lord, they didn't really understand, did they? Not until later. How could they? For no one to this day really comprehends the full meaning of your Cross because no one else has had to bear such an awful burden as universal sin for all ages. But you, Lord, and the people around me who have lost loved ones understand my pain and the tears I cry. Help me, Lord, to admit how much I hurt and to resolve to do something about it before it does something to me. Through Jesus I pray. Amen.

Feel
your pain

It's O.K. to be in pain. It's O.K. to hurt when death takes someone you love. Sometimes you may wish you had no feelings, for then you would not be hurting so. But if that were true, neither could you have loved that person so dearly. Love and pain go hand in hand, for they proceed from the same capacity to feel. We find that fact of life hard to accept, but there's another to consider: just as it's O.K. to love, it's O.K. to feel the pain that comes from loving and losing.

So, accept your pain as part of you. There is nothing wrong with hurting. It does not make you any less a person but more so, because the pain you feel right now is evidence that you have dared to love. Don't deny your hurt. Let yourself experience it just as much as you let yourself experience the love.

Feel the pain. Don't back away from it. But don't lie down in it either. Instead, *lean* into it, keeping your feet on solid ground.

Lean into your pain. Experience its feelings. Cry if you feel the need to; don't hold back the tears that beg to flow. Tell someone how much you hurt and what it feels like. Tell him why you feel that way. Say what's on your mind and heart. Get it out in the open, or you'll never face it and deal with it.

You'll feel a blessed relief each time you do this. But remember this: express only those thoughts and feelings you need to express at that moment. Don't overdo. Once you've opened up your grief, don't force its outward flow. Instead, let it flow as it will, and lean into the pain as much as you can without falling into it. Then, when you intuitively know that the time has come to stop, stop. Even if your listener encourages you on, stop. Only you know what your limits are.

Psalm 31:9, 14–15
> Be merciful to me, O LORD, for I am in distress;
> > my eyes grow weak with sorrow,
> > my soul and my body with grief. . . .
> But I trust in you, O LORD;
> > I say, "You are my God."
> My times are in your hands.

1 Peter 4:19
> So then, those who suffer according to God's will should commit themselves to their faithful Creator and continue to do good.

Dear Lord, all my life I've tried to avoid as much pain as possible. No one in his right mind invites pain, much less "leans" into it! But the pain is already there, isn't it? And that's what you wanted me to see. That makes more sense than fighting it, I admit. But, Lord, all my defenses make me want to struggle to stand straight and not let it get to me. Those defenses tell me that if I let myself feel the depths of my sorrow, I will hurt even more and for no good reason. "Why torture yourself?" they ask. You must help me, God, to at least give it a try. I want to trust my emotional health to you just as I trust my physical well-being to you when I am sick. I want to believe that if I try leaning into my pain, you will guard me from falling into it and taking on more than I can bear at any one time. Help me to trust you in this way. My times are indeed in your hand. In the power of the Savior's victorious name. Amen.

Take inventory of your pain

Pain is a package word. It's a bundle of feelings, all miserable, intense, acutely felt. And the pain of grief is more than just sadness or melancholia. Rather, it is usually a combination of complex emotions, feelings which most people uninitiated to deep grief do not realize are there.

Have you explored inside your pain to see what you really feel that hurts so much? Do you know your feelings by name? It's the thing to do in grief work. Feel the pain; express it outwardly in a positive, harmless way; examine the feelings that are there, and name them. What is there for you to see?

Perhaps guilt. Remorse for things that happened or things that didn't. Actions, words, or feelings that transpired between you and the one who is no longer here for you to say "I'm sorry" to. Things you neglected to do or say.

And what about anger—that feeling of silent rage and bitterness that hangs over your head like a dark and ominous cloud, that resentment you are harboring inside you?

It's possible, too, that fear is there. An unnamed uneasiness or anxiety. A very frightening possibility you're all too well aware of.

And would you believe jealousy? Disgruntlement and envy you sometimes may feel when you look at the living. The feeling that you've been dealt with unjustly, especially in comparison to them.

There's also the feeling of loneliness. That over-whelming emptiness of isolation and desertion. That lack of security and love from another.

These could be some of the feelings wrapped up in your private package of pain. The deeper, more specific feelings that cause the hurt.

Take inventory of what you feel. Not to make yourself more miserable, even though such an exercise will be uncomfortable, but to get on with the business of working through grief.

Romans 8:17
> Now if we are children [of God], then we are heirs—heirs of God and co-heirs with Christ, if indeed we share in his sufferings in order that we may also share in his glory.

Psalm 145:18
> The LORD is near to all who call on him,
>   to all who call on him in truth.

O Lord, you always insist upon the truth. And I usually had rather settle for the comforts of not knowing, because the truth is often frightening to me. Or at least the prospect of knowing it is. As I understand it, these feelings that have been named may very well be some of the "trolls" that are hiding in the shadows of this tunnel. I don't like them, Lord, and I don't look forward to meeting them and knowing they are part of me! But I must take the risk of encountering them if I'm to get through the tunnel, mustn't I? So, give me your hand, Father, and take me through my suffering by means of the power and energy of truth. In your name. Amen.

Grieve naturally

Guilt, anger, fear, jealousy, loneliness—whatever the feelings (and there may be others I've not named), they need to be faced instead of denied, expressed instead of suppressed or repressed, and dealt with constructively instead of destructively.

You may not be proud of them. Some may embarrass you. All of them will hurt to some degree when you try to deal with them. But if you realize that it's all right to have them, then it's easier to be rid of them.

It's O.K. to have those feelings. You'd be an extraordinary person if you didn't have at least some of them. Every one of us is human and subject to having any or all of the human emotions, especially in time of personal crisis.

But it's not O.K. to keep them, because it's unhealthy to possess them to the point that they come to possess you. They can gnaw at you and actually make you ill. They can fester inside you, making you and those around you miserable. You must not deceive yourself into thinking they will magically go away with time, or that you can conquer them while they remain inside. They'll only show up sooner or later in another form, expressing themselves outwardly in a harmful fashion. And you'll have a greater price to pay. Make no mistake about it: in one way or another, grief will work its way out. That's as predictable as tomorrow morning's sunrise.

So, let those grief-feelings come out in the most practical and beneficial way possible—the natural way. And the sooner, the better. Grieve now, before your feelings are forced to take alternative routes.

Proverbs 28:13
> He who conceals his sins does not prosper,
>> but whoever confesses and renounces them
>>> finds mercy.

James 5:16
> Therefore confess your sins ‘to each other and pray for each other so that you may be healed.

Oh me, Lord. I never thought of grief in terms of sin. It almost seems preposterous! But I am a Christian, and Christians are more likely to accept the facts of sin than anyone else these days. Come to think of it, some of these feelings discussed here could have to do with sin. Real guilt infers there is sin. Anger can be sinful, I guess. Surely envy is sin. And when you think of how these feelings, whether sinful or not, can affect your life negatively, I suppose that's a sin because it means you are hurting yourself. Are any of these things in me? Show me, Lord, if they are, and give me the grace I will surely need to face them and deal rightly with them. In the name of Jesus. Amen.

Identify your guilt

Quite often the pain of sorrow involves guilt. Sometimes it's bona fide guilt. More often than not, however, it's false.

If there is not the slightest particle of guilt among your grief feelings, consider yourself fortunate and rare. Because it appears to be a prevalent thing. Something tragic happens, and someone somewhere is going to feel guilty. That's just the way human beings are.

The important thing is to know what you may be dealing with and what to do about it. If guilt is part of your package of pain, is it real or imagined?

Real guilt is the fact of having committed some wrong or having willfully and consciously refused to do some right regarding the deceased. It can be recognized only by rational thinking based in truth. Is it a fact that you are truly culpable of what you feel guilty for? Did you in fact willfully and knowingly break the law of God and/or man? If so, you can't make amends to the person you've sinned against. But you can seek forgiveness from God. So, the thing that must be done to be free of this guilt is to confess the sin, seek God's pardon, accept his forgiveness, and then—and here's the hard part—forgive yourself.

But false guilt is quite another matter. It's the "if only's," a useless, irrational exercise in self-punishment. "If only I had visited her in the last few days of her life." "If only I had been the one driving the car that day." "If only I had known he was so ill." If only, if only, if only—a circle that won't end unless you put a stop to it. And you can when you realize that your guilt is not true but stems from irrational and/or wishful thinking. Stop thinking those thoughts; stop accusing yourself; stop telling yourself that you are to blame. Replace those thoughts with positive ones. And with the truth.

Psalm 103:8, 11–14
> The LORD is compassionate and gracious,
>   slow to anger, abounding in love. . . .
> For as high as the heavens are above the earth,
>   so great is his love for those who fear him;
> as far as the east is from the west,
>   so far has he removed our transgressions
>   from us.
> As a father has compassion on his children,
>   so the LORD has compassion on those who
>   fear him;
> for he knows how we are formed,
>   he remembers that we are dust.

Psalm 51:6, 10
> Surely you desire truth in the inner parts;
>   you teach me wisdom in the inmost place. . . .
> Create in me a pure heart, O God,
>   and renew a steadfast spirit within me.

My Lord, I can see how guilt is part of my grief. I don't quite understand it all yet, but at least I am aware of it. Convict me of the things that are truly wrong, and help me to accept your forgiveness and forgive myself. Show me the false guilt that plagues me; expose it for what it really is and help me to put it away and forget it. I place all my guilt, true and false, at the foot of your Cross. Help me to dispose of it in the necessary ways and be free of it forever. Through Christ who died for me. Amen.

Understand your anger

You've probably seen it happen before. A child is playing with a favorite toy, and suddenly there's an accident in which he gets hurt. What is his first reaction? Most likely, to get angry and kick the toy that's hurt him.

It seems to be a natural inclination of human beings to respond with anger at something or somebody whenever we get hurt. Anger, because we operate on the principle of cause and effect. Our pain is so great that the blame for it has to be fixed, or so our thinking goes. And if we don't place the blame upon ourselves and feel guilty for it, we're apt to place it elsewhere.

When someone you love dies, anger can rise up within you and be directed at any of several directions. Do you feel angry? At what or whom? These are the questions to ask yourself so that you can conquer the feeling rather than allow it to conquer you.

You can be angry at the means of death. A river or lake, the airplane or the automobile, the sport of hunting or car racing, or Mother Nature and her capricious ways, for example. In your mind, one of these, or the like, may be the guilty "culprit" to blame for your loved one's death. But think rationally now. None of these is a murderer; none of these can will to kill. Are you really angry at such an object or at the human factor involved in them?

Is it a person or group of people whom you judge responsible for the loss of life? The ambulance driver who didn't get to the hospital in time? Your husband's buddies who invited him to go hunting with them? The company which transferred your son-in-law to the Gulf Coast where hurricanes strike? The teenage boy who was driving your daughter to a movie that night? Think only of what is true in such situations as these. The person or persons you blame and are angry with—did they knowingly and willfully kill the one you love?

And what about the person or persons you know without doubt to have been negligent or engaged in wrongdoing? The drunken driver, the employees at work who were constantly creating stressful situations, the man who robbed the service station, the doctor who was careless. In this kind of situation, the key word is forgiveness. Difficult though it may be, forgiveness is your only release from an anger that will bring a physical, mental, and spiritual toll upon your life. A heavy toll which you, not the guilty party, will have to pay. You've got to consciously work at being willing to forgive. There's simply no other way.

And could you ever be angry at the one you've lost? Angry with him because he ceased to live? Widows in grief often feel this way. "Why did he have to die just when I need him most? I've got these debts to pay and these children to raise alone—why did he have to die *now*?" Although it is not at all rational, it is natural to feel angry when one you had counted on is no longer here to meet his responsibilities. So admit it, express it, and forgive yourself. You probably feel guilty for feeling that way, and that does you no good.

Then there's anger you may feel toward God. "How could he let such a thing happen?" "Why would he deprive such a good and talented person from living out the rest of his life?" It does no good to swallow this anger every time someone mentions "God's will" or that a Christian shouldn't be angry with God. *Tell* God exactly how you feel. He knows anyway, and he wants you to be honest with him because when you are, you must be honest with yourself. But while you're telling him, remember, too, that it is vitally important to also ask his graciousness in helping you to understand and accept his ways. It does little good to tell God you're angry with him if you don't give him permission to help you overcome it.

Matthew 6:14–15

"For if you forgive men when they sin against you, your heavenly Father will also forgive you. But if you do not forgive men their sins, your Father will not forgive your sins."

Ephesians 4:31–32

Get rid of all bitterness, rage and anger, brawling and slander, along with every form of malice. Be kind and compassionate to one another, forgiving each other, just as in Christ God forgave you.

Yes, Lord, I do feel some anger. But it's so hard to face! I know I'm not "supposed" to feel angry because I am a Christian. It therefore eludes me when I try to define it. Too, I feel "justified" in feeling it. Oh, what a mess, Lord! What am I to do? Teach me about forgiveness, God, and help me to see more clearly the error of my ways. I give to you what little willingness I have to face the anger. Increase it so that I can do, through you, what I must do to be rid of it. In the strength of my Redeemer's name I pray. Amen.

19

Face
those new fears

FEAR—a powerful little word. It can make you anxious at the very least. At the most, it can immobilize.

Are you afraid? Of what, then? Being alone with no one to love you? Meeting financial obligations? Things that go bump in the night? Having another child after having lost one? Getting a job for the first time in twenty-five years? Meeting people of the opposite sex? Loving and losing again?

Most fears that arise out of having lost a loved one are irrational. They come from such thoughts as these: I can't possibly make it alone. . . . I can never love again. . . . I cannot survive another loss like this one.

If you're telling yourself one or all of these, you are not dealing in truth. You *can* face life and make it without the person you've lost. You *can* love another person again. You *can* survive another loss.

Change your thinking to the positive and the true: I *want* to make it in life even without the one I love, for my life hasn't ended yet. . . . I *want* to open myself to loving again because I have the need to love and to be loved. . . . I *want* to take the risk of losing which comes with loving because I know it's better to love and lose than not to love at all.

Identify your fears. Find out what it is you're telling yourself that makes you feel afraid. Look at it squarely for what fear is: just a feeling and no reliable guarantee of future events.

And then go out and get involved in life, one step at a time. All you need is a smidgen of courage in order to make that first step. You'll be surprised to see that courage has a way of growing with the second, third, and fourth.

And whatever you do in trying to deal with any kind of fear, don't forget the power of faith. Tell the One in whom "all things hold together" your specific fears. Ask for the help of his enabling Spirit. You and he can do wonders in overcoming fear.

Psalm 46:1–3

> God is our refuge and strength,
>   an ever present help in trouble.
> Therefore we will not fear, though the earth
>   give way
>   and the mountains fall into the heart of the sea,
>   though its waters roar and foam
>   and the mountains quake with their surging.

Philippians 4:6–7

> Do not be anxious about anything, but in every-thing, by prayer and petition, with thanksgiving, present your requests to God. And the peace of God, which transcends all understanding, will guard your hearts and your minds in Christ Jesus.

You know me inside and out, don't you, Lord? I go on and on about how much I depend on you and all the while I'm worrying or afraid. So many little anxieties, some of which have been part of me long before grief set in and some which grief has caused. And yes, I am afraid of loving and losing again. It hurts so much to lose, Lord! I don't ever want to feel this way again. So I try to marshal my defenses from ever again being in the position where I could lose. But that's silly, isn't it? I can't protect myself from that. Instead, I should be giving all my fears to you. But it's so difficult to do, Father! Increase my faith in you and give me your peace of mind. Through Christ my Lord. Amen.

20

Recognize your jealousy

You may think that it takes a petty and selfish person to feel jealous toward the living. Still, it is a grief-reaction, and most people in deep grief feel it to some degree. It could be so slight in you that you don't easily recognize it. But if it's there, it really should come out. It's another one of those feelings that can help keep you dissatisfied with the circumstances of your life.

Jealousy is never pretty. That's why we try to hide it with rationalizations. But no rationalization can justify it, especially when what you're jealous of is the fact that others have life while your loved one has been deprived of it.

"I would have been a good mother to my child, but look at how she neglects hers. Why would God take mine when she apparently doesn't even want hers!"

"My nephew was such a good, decent young man. He had so much to offer, and his life was only beginning when it ended. But look at his father—a drunk, a wife-beater, a ne'er-do-well. Why couldn't it have been him? No one would have missed him for long."

"That boy must not have had any sense. It was he who was so insistent on driving in the ice and snow when they could have easily stopped for the night. If someone had to die, it should have been him instead of my son. Why, he didn't get even so much as a scratch upon his body!"

"I just can't bear to be around George and Meg any more. She's such a good wife, but he treats her like dirt sometimes. Bob would have never done me that way. Oh why, Lord, did you take my Bob so early when there are so many Georges in this world?"

Recognize yourself? Own it, then. Confess it aloud. Ask God's forgiveness for wanting to assume his responsibilitiy for who leaves this life when. Then, forgive yourself—you're only human. Do this, and you'll be better equipped to handle the feeling of jealousy should it raise its selfish head again. Because you know it now for what it really is.

James 4:12
> There is only one Lawgiver and Judge, the one who is able to save and destroy. But you—who are you to judge your neighbor?

Matthew 5:45
> "He causes his sun to shine on the evil and the good, and sends rain on the righteous and the unrighteous."

Dear God, I am so ashamed. I didn't realize it, but I've been guilty of this one, too. Please give me the measure of grace I need to turn from this way of thinking about my neighbor. Please forgive me for criticizing you and your decisions. Help me to remember who you are and who I am. And help me to be glad that all justice is in your hands and that you will dispense it according to your good and perfect will without my having to understand why. Increase my trust in you and your control. In the name of Jesus Christ. Amen.

21

Reach out in your loneliness

Any quality love relationship between two people involves investment. No matter how you were related to the one you grieve for, you gave part of yourself to that person and vice versa. Then death came along. The relationship, as you had known it, was disrupted and dissolved. Part of yourself died with that person. And now a major source of giving and receiving is cut off, terminated, gone.

Too, this kind of relationship involves mutual need. You had need of that person's continuing love and support. He had need of yours. And you also needed to be needed by him. But now these things have vanished from your life.

You still feel the compulsion to give love in these two ways as well as to receive it from the relationship you had. But one-half of it is missing now. And part of the anguish of your grief is that you feel left behind, alone in the relationship that still exists in your mind.

All this means that part of your mourning is for yourself. You've been deprived of a significant relationship which you still feel the need and desire to have. You know that no one can ever be that same child or friend or mate to you, even though you may have another. No other can give himself to you, need you, or love you in quite the same way.

So, if you feel deserted, desolate, and lonely, realize that while it's natural for you to grieve for your-

self in that way, it's also unhealthy to let this feeling
sink in until it has a firm hold on your mind. It's unhealthy to think and believe that you can never love
another so deeply. Or that no other can love you so
well. Or that you don't want to need or invest your
life in someone else ever again for fear of the pain and
disappointment of losing one more time. And, most
pathetic of all, it's unhealthy to refuse to accept the
fact that your loved one is indeed gone from this life.

I'm not saying, don't miss the one you love. That
is neither possible nor desirable. Nor am I saying,
don't talk about him, your relationship, and what he
meant to you. You really should, for this is part of
expressing grief.

But I do want to remind you that life is more than
just one relationship. You have a relationship with
God, with yourself, and with an unlimited number of
others. Enliven those relationships. Commune with
the Lord . . . get to know yourself better . . . open
yourself to the prospect of new and more meaningful
friendships.

You are not really alone. Unless you make it so.

Matthew 22:37–40

> Jesus replied: " 'Love the Lord your God with all
> your heart and with all your soul and with all
> your mind.' This is the first and greatest com-
> mandment. And the second is like it: 'Love your
> neighbor as yourself.' All the Law and the Proph-
> ets hang on these two commandments."

1 Corinthians 13:1–3

> If I speak in the tongues of men and of angels,
> but have not love, I am only a resounding gong
> or a clanging cymbal. If I have the gift of
> prophecy and can fathom all mysteries and all
> knowledge, and if I have a faith that can move
> mountains, but have not love, I am nothing. If I

give all I possess to the poor and surrender my body to the flames, but have not love, I gain nothing.

Dear Lord in heaven, this is the most terrible part of grief. I miss the one I love so much. I can hardly stand it, it hurts so bad! It's as if I'd lost a limb: I've been so used to having it; I need it in order to be able to function as well as I have before; I feel the phantom pains in a part of my body that's no longer there! Help me to adjust to the loss. Help me to adapt my life to the absence. Heal the pain of longing to have the one I love with me again. And, in the meantime, give me the courage to reach out to others so that I can give to them and they to me, for this loneliness is more than I can bear. In Jesus' blessed name. Amen.

22

Make God your best friend

God is the ultimate in friends. There is no other who knows better the person you are and the person you can become. He knows more about you than the number of hairs upon your head. He also knows the psychology behind every thought, feeling, and action that is individual to your personality. He knows "where you're coming from" and how to help you get to where you need to go in order to heal.

But more than that, God's love for you is greater than any human's. And he wants more good for you than you or any other mortal could ever imagine.

Too, he's more faithful than any other friend. You can count on him to keep his promises when you claim them. It's impossible for him not to keep them when they are rightly claimed.

Sometimes, however, we find all these things hard to believe. We think they must not be so. Because we look at God and what he does or allows to happen with near-sighted eyes. We can only see as far as what we ourselves want or think should happen. So, we judge God, calling him unfair, unloving, and unfaithful. And all this stems from thinking that we know better than the omnipotent, omniscient God of the universe. Or that we are capable of greater love than the one who gave himself for sinners, including our very own selves.

But when we respond to his ever-extended hand of friendship by trusting and obeying him, things begin to happen. Good things. Joyful things. Large and small miracles that are continuing proofs of his steadfast love and true concern for us in the here and now.

And then it doesn't matter if we don't fully comprehend his ways. Then, it's sufficient just to understand that God is good and that he loves us in a way no one's ever loved us before, or ever will.

Micah 6:8
> He has showed you, O man, what is good.
>   And what does the LORD require of you?
> To act justly and to love mercy
>   and to walk humbly with your God.

John 14:23
> Jesus replied, "If anyone loves me, he will obey my teaching. My Father will love him, and we will come to him and make our home with him."

Dear God, how much I need you! If there is only one thing I'm learning about you and me in all of this, it is that I am totally dependent upon you! Lord, I want you to be more "at home" in me. I want you to be more than my help in times of trouble; I want you to be my best friend, too. Help me to allow you to do that. Help me to learn more of what it means to walk humbly with you. And I will praise your name and give you the glory, for you have been so good and kind to me. In his name and for his sake. Amen.

Tune in to your self-talk

What you feel depends on what you think or tell yourself. Sometimes what you think is true. At other times you may exaggerate or twist the truth until you're telling yourself an untruth and believing it.

For example, you could be thinking, "I'll never be happy again," which in turn makes you feel unhappy. The truth is, however, that there is every possibility in the world you can be happy again. There's no law that says you are hereby excluded forever from the pursuit of happiness. While you cannot regain what you've lost and be happy for that reason, the fact remains that you can be happy for other reasons, other relationships. That is the truth. And if you tell yourself that, you won't feel so unhappy.

How do you recognize faulty, irrational thinking that creates all those negative feelings you can do just as well without? Here are a few guidelines:

1. Is what I'm telling myself the truth of the matter?
2. When I say "I can't," do I in truth mean "I won't" or "I don't want to"?
3. When I use an absolute term like "all the time," "never," "should," "no one," and "everybody," am I really being truthful?
4. Am I attributing the cause of my feelings to someone else or something outside myself instead of acknowledging that I am the one who's responsible for what I feel?

Remember, you are responsible for your feelings as well as your actions because both proceed from what you choose to think. And if your thinking must rely on someone else's thoughts, let them come from the mind of Jesus Christ alone.

Be responsible for yourself; be truthful with yourself. These are essential to creative, productive, constructive grief work.

Proverbs 20:5
> The purposes of a man's heart are deep waters,
> > but a man of understanding draws them out.

Proverbs 23:23
> Buy the truth and do not sell it;
> > get wisdom, discipline and understanding.

Can all this be true, Lord? Do I sometimes tell myself lies? Do I dodge responsibility for myself? And are these things the roots of some of my problems? I'm sure the answer to these questions could be "yes." But I don't see it, Lord. I guess I've had too much success in deceiving myself, too much to readily recognize the subtle ways in which I do it. Instill in me a new value for the truth, dear God. Reveal to me those things I so unwittingly do so that I may acknowledge them, accept them as part of me, and change them for the better. In Christ's name. Amen.

24

Make your mind work *for* you

Your emotional attitude toward life and all its circumstances, large and small, good and bad, depends upon your established patterns of thinking. This is so because what you think about a certain situation determines what you feel about it.

The people who find life hard to cope with are those who respond to their difficulties with patterns of irrational and/or negative thought. They tell themselves things that aren't necessarily true. Their thoughts dwell on the bad they see in a situation. Their expectations of growth, happiness, and the good that can result from adversity are very low. And they usually get what they expect.

But have you ever noticed that some people seem to just naturally overcome their troubles and live fuller, richer lives than would ordinarily seem possible? Those around them call them "brave," "strong," and "of great faith." And most observers say, "I don't know how they do it!"

These "winners" are indeed brave, strong, and of great faith because a basic element in their personality allows the Lord to make them so. That element is their "mind set," patterns of thinking which are more rational than irrational, more positive than negative. It is no particular talent or blessing, no certain inborn quality, but merely a way of thinking.

If you are one of those who says, "I don't know how they do it," consider this fact. All you have to do is to work on changing your old habits of thinking. Then, you'll not only know how, but you can do it, too.

Write down the negative feelings you often have in a particular kind of situation that frequently repeats itself. Then complete this sentence for each feeling: I feel____ because____. Now, go back and look at the "because" for each one. Is it true? An absolute fact? Remember, the "because" is what you're telling yourself (your thought) which in turn creates the "I feel" (your feeling). Are you misleading yourself with half-truths? Non-truths? Twisted truths?

Next, replace any irrational (false) thought with a rational (true) one. Perhaps the feeling is still there because what you've told yourself is true. If it is, test the "because" by asking yourself, "Is this the only fact operating here? Is there a more positive one I can substitute for it?"

Let me give you an example of how this exercise works.

I'm washing dishes one morning when I realize that I'm in a bad mood again. I want to be rid of it, so I ask myself, "What is it that makes me feel this way?"

This answer comes to mind: "I feel angry because John made me so mad when I went into his room after he left for school and found his dirty sox lying on the floor again. He never picks them up like he knows he should."

Having identified what seems to be the problem, I then give it the rational test: "First of all, this 'because' is not true; John cannot 'make' me angry. Rather, I became angry of my own will when I saw the sox lying on the floor. Furthermore, 'never' is not true because John sometimes does remember to pick them up. I'm just such a perfectionist that I only notice when he doesn't. And third, I am not being reasonable when I use the word 'should' because I am forgetting that John is a seven-year-old boy, and I cannot expect him to perform like an adult who has already been trained and knows better."

Then I have to face the fact of what I'm really telling myself when I get so angry at John about the sox: "The truth is, I feel angry when John forgets to pick up his sox because I automatically take his negligence personally. I think that he doesn't care enough about me, his poor, hard-working mother who is trying her best as a parent alone to make a good home for him, to help keep the house in order. And that's not true either."

That clears things up somewhat, but I still can't stand dirty sox on the floor that I have to pick up myself. And I can't afford the guilt that's creeping in on me because I resent them having been thrown there. So, I try for the positive: "I'm looking at one single failing of John when there are so many good things I could think about where John and a clean house are concerned. I could think about the facts that he takes out the garbage, helps clear the table after meals, and lends his little sister a hand in picking up her toys every night. And most of the time he does these things without question or complaint. Come to think of it, I have reason to be proud of my son. I feel loving towards him now because he helps me in so many ways. Even if he forgets sometimes to put his sox in the dirty clothes hamper."

Changing the pattern of irrational/negative thinking to rational/positive thinking takes conscious effort. It means re-training your old patterns of thinking. But you can do it if you really want to.

The next time you find yourself deluged with the thoughts of a bad mood, try this exercise. Write it all down so you can see it. And with time, you *will* change your way of thinking. And your feelings, too.

Philippians 4:8
> Finally, brothers, whatever is true, whatever is noble, whatever is right, whatever is pure, whatever is lovely, whatever is admirable—if anything is excellent or praiseworthy—think about such things.

1 Timothy 4:15
> Be diligent in these matters; give yourself wholly to them, so that everyone may see your progress.

I must confess, dear Lord, that I may talk big about making changes, but when it comes down to brass tacks, I really don't want to make them. Change my way of thinking? Why, Lord, I've been thinking this way for many years! I just don't see how this can work for me. And you already know all the excuses I have to offer, especially the one that says, "Well, this could be so for others, but I'm the way I am, and I can't change because God just made me this way." But you really aren't responsible for the "way I am," are you? I have made me so. And if that's the truth of the matter, help me to believe that I can also instigate the changes that are desirable. But I need your help so much, God. Let your Holy Spirit work the necessary changes in my way of thinking, and help me to be willing to give him free rein to perform this kind of miracle in me. Through Jesus my Lord. Amen.

25

Do something constructive

Sometimes rational/positive thinking doesn't come easy. You know what is rational; you know what is positive. You write them down and look at them; you know it is best to incorporate them into your thinking. But somehow you seem unable to follow through.

Sometimes you just don't want to think rationally or positively even when you know how. Did you catch the key words there? You don't want to.

That's O.K. It's O.K. not to want to every now and then, as long as you tell yourself two things in addition to the I-don't-want-to: I will do something else constructive instead of sitting here all depressed and blue, and I will not give up on rational/positive thinking altogether.

What is there to do? Do the kitchen cabinets need new shelf paper? Or the car a wash and wax job? What about that novel you've heard people rave about? Why not go buy it or check it out of the library? Make yourself a new dress. Plan a surprise outing for the kids. Exercise a creative talent. Go see a movie that's light and entertaining. Visit or call a friend in whose company you take delight.

Better yet, do something for someone else. Visit a person who's lonely. Take fresh flowers from your garden to a shut-in. Bake a cake for that neighbor who's often done thoughtful little things for you. You've probably received much ministry in Christ's name from others. Be on the giving end for a change.

And the mood will pass. The feelings won't be taken

care of, necessarily (though you may discover help with them comes when you're serving others.) Just don't mislead yourself into thinking that activity and lots of it is the answer to every grief problem, or that rational/positive thinking are unnecessary exercises. These things aren't true. Don't fool yourself into thinking they are.

Luke 6:38

> "Give, and it will be given to you. A good measure, pressed down, shaken together and running over, will be poured into your lap."

2 Corinthians 1:3–4

> Praise be to the God and Father of our Lord Jesus Christ, the Father of compassion and the God of all comfort, who comforts us in all our troubles, so that we can comfort those in any trouble with the comfort we ourselves have received from God.

O thank you, Lord, that I don't have to be perfect in grief work! I don't know why I thought I had to be. Even with your helping me, I'm bound to slip behind sometimes. Just help me, Lord, to make my "time off" from grief work productive time. Make me a channel of your blessing to others. Help me to give even when I don't want to give to myself. In the name of Jesus Christ. Amen.

26

Be friends with your subconscious

The subconscious—that part of the mind that lies below the surface of conscious thinking—is a curious, mysterious thing. Particularly in the midst of deep grief, it can play tricks on the conscious mind. Things you aren't aware of surface now and then, often in disguised forms and leaving you to wonder about your progress in grief or even your sanity. And just as quickly as they come, they usually disappear, defying all attempts of logic and reason to understand what happened and why.

Old memories you thought you had dealt with constructively, or at least had grown used to, can return in full force at any moment. They may come even when the one you've lost seems farthest from your mind. Or they can be triggered by stimuli you haven't encountered in your grief before, like an old, favorite song you haven't heard in years. Or an old friend of your loved one you haven't seen or thought of since before the death. Or a stranger whose looks, speech, and mannerisms bear an uncanny resemblance to the one who is no longer living.

Memory can also play what seems to be a harsher and more cruel prank. You can try to remember your loved one's face and draw a complete blank. You can try to recall the sound of that voice or that laugh and fail.

And then there's recurrence of the initial shock of learning about the death. Say it's been a year or so since your loss. You've been getting better since then. Suddenly out of nowhere comes the shock and disbelief that the one you love is really dead. "Did it really happen?" you ask yourself, knowing full well, intellectually, that it did. "I can hardly believe it's so. Even now that so much has changed without him, I can hardly believe it's true."

And as if all this weren't enough, there's the problem of disturbing dreams. Pleasant dreams of the deceased you can take some comfort in. But not the same confusing dream happening again and again, or the recurrence of different dreams that carry the same unsettling theme, such as alienation between you and the one you've lost.

With all of these, just remember that the subconscious mind is trying to tell you something your conscious mind isn't aware of or refuses to acknowledge. It may be that the message is simply, "You are still in grief; you haven't finished yet." It may be, "There's something important that you have left undone or haven't adequately dealt with in your grief work." Or it could be, "There's a real, urgent problem here that needs attention."

Whatever the message (and only you can decipher it), the important things for you to bear in mind at times like these are:

1. Don't feel guilty or "weird." Such things happen all the time to others in grief. You are not alone in them.

2. Don't let yourself become frightened of the subconscious or unnecessarily worried about it.

3. Listen to your subconscious. Learn how it speaks to you and what its symbols mean. It's your mind; the symbols will be distinctly yours.

4. Discuss the things that leave you extremely upset and disturbed with a friend or a professional, for it's possible they can help you unravel the mystery.

5. Do whatever you realize you must do in order to take care of any problem the subconscious suggests. Then it will be satisfied and cease to send its message.

Daniel 2:22
> He reveals deep and hidden things;
> he knows what lies in darkness,
> and light dwells with him.

Philippians 4:19
> And my God will meet all your needs according to his
> glorious riches in Christ Jesus.

Dear Father, I hardly understand my conscious thinking, much less my deeper thoughts. I am so glad that someone who loves me and who is higher than I knows them all quite well. Even though I am perplexed sometimes by the way my mind works, I am convinced that you can help me understand what I need to know and am capable of knowing in any particular instance. So, I need your help in untangling the mysterious parts of me that bother me. Reveal them to me, as you will, so that I can understand what you'd have me know, and give me what I need to handle them well. In the power of Jesus' name. Amen.

27

Love yourself

Some days just don't go right at all. It seems everything you do or say comes out wrong. The stress that builds with each little mistake, misfortune, and disappointment is compounded by the fact that you haven't quite recovered from your grief. Tension adds to tension until you're knotted by nerves and feelings of inadequacy.

Finally, it begins to happen. The pressure of the day becomes too much, and you do and say unkind things you immediately regret but find so difficult to contain. And the worse part of it all is that the object of your actions and words is usually someone you love.

After you've calmed down a bit, perhaps you offer an apology. But that doesn't make you feel any better. In fact, you're apt to think you're a fairly loathsome human being. And no protestations of affirmation and love from the one on whom you've vented your feelings is likely to change your mental picture of an ugly, detestable you.

So, what can you do? You can continue to silently berate and belittle yourself until you're further depressed. You can feel sorry for yourself because you're having such a hard time. You can even punish yourself in some external fashion because you know you "deserve" it.

You can choose any or all of these options and feel justified in doing so. Or you can stop and remember whose child you are. That's the hardest thing to do, but it's the best. Because, you see, a worthless image of yourself, no matter how vile and hopeless, can't hold its own when compared to the view the Lord has of you.

Of all the living things he created to inhabit this earth, he chose you to be one of the only kind who are conscious of him, can communicate with him, and can know him in a one-to-one relationship. He must have had good reason for doing that, for the Lord wastes nothing nor leaves it to "accident." With that thought in mind, who can honestly and with all good conscience degrade this wonderful, unique product of the Creative Genius behind the entire universe?

And think of this. He also chose you to be a child of the King, a member in ever-good-standing of the eternal Kingdom of God. You have the Kingdom within you now, and someday you will actually see it and be able to grasp it totally with your whole being. It will surely happen because you are a joint heir in the Kingdom of the Living God with Jesus Christ himself.

But you have not gained the Kingdom within and to come on the merit of your own performances in life. That would be impossible, for you are the maker of mistakes and wrong choices. This bad day you've had is proof enough of that.

And if, when you remember these things, you begin to think, "Yes, I *am* a bad apple. I don't even deserve the love of God," you will still continue to think ill of yourself.

I can imagine the Lord really getting upset every time one of us thinks that way. I can hear him replying, "So you don't merit my love, eh? That's no news to me! I know you don't deserve a single ounce of it, but I give it to you freely anyway. So, how dare you tell me that the blood of my sinless Son wasn't enough for you? How dare you suggest that I shouldn't have bothered? How can you sit there in your self-absorption and deny the worth I have given you by refusing to love the person *I* love enough to have died for?"

Sobering, isn't it? Grace is not a one-time thing, thank God, but a fountain of cleansing and justification, forever flowing to keep us worthy in God's sight to be his own.

It follows, then, that refusing to love ourselves as God loves us is sin. It's a twisted kind of pride that mocks the life, death, and resurrection of the One whose name we bear. Furthermore, it belittles all the efforts of our brothers and sisters throughout the ages who have kept alive the Christian faith so that it could be passed along to us. And those were no paltry attempts to preserve and foster the faith. Very often they were acts of raw courage wracked with a kind of suffering you and I can't begin to fathom because we don't have to experience it, thanks to them.

Remember always your spiritual heritage and inheritance. A continuing awareness of them helps you to love yourself. Not out of self-deception, for you can acknowledge your faults and failings and still love yourself. Not out of guilt, either, for the One who makes us worthy of the Kingdom knows we will err and stands ever ready to forgive our mistakes and help us learn from them.

Give it a try the next time you are putting yourself down, and you'll find that when you love yourself because of whose child you are, you'll be loving God. When you accept yourself, imperfections and all, because of who you are in his sight, you'll be glorifying the Lord Jesus Christ who's given you your identity in himself.

James 3:9–12

With the tongue we praise our Lord and Father, and with it we curse men, who have been made in God's likeness. Out of the mouth come praise and cursing. My brothers, this should not be. Can both fresh water and salt water flow from the same spring? My brothers, can a fig tree bear olives, or a grapevine bear figs? Neither can a salt spring produce fresh water.

1 Peter 1:18–19

For you know that it was not with perishable things such as silver and gold that you were redeemed from the empty way of life handed down to you from your forefathers, but with the precious blood of Christ, a lamb without blemish or defect.

O Lord, so often I'm guilty of not loving myself. And while it may not be that my tongue curses others, it is true that my thoughts do belittle and degrade one God has made and saved. And that one is me. The next time I forget my worth in your sight, or my inheritance in Christ, or my Christian heritage, bring to my mind the image of the salty spring. Help me to remember whose I am and the price paid for me. Help me to love myself in the way you want me to. Keep it ever in my mind that I cannot obey your two great commandments if I don't love myself. Thank you, Lord, that I am something truly valuable in your eyes and that you've given me your identity through Christ. Make my self-image one that will continually reflect the glory and honor of my Lord Jesus. In his name. Amen.

28

Let God love you

Let God love you. Let him be more than your Savior and the Lord of your life. More than authority figure, a help in present trouble, your protector and provider. Let him be these things for you, yes, but understand that there's so much more he wants to bring into his relationship with you.

Open wide your total being to him. Let him enter fully into your spiritual and mental acceptance of him. Let him be the Lover of your soul.

One of the primary things we look for most in life is love. Someone special to relate to us in the most caring, loving way. A friend or mate who will always understand us, support us, be true to us, and give unselfishly to us. One with whom we can dare to be our real selves, devoid of all the roles and games we play, and who loves us anyway with a deep and loyal affection. One who will allow us to love him in the same way.

Sometimes we are fortunate enough to find that friend or spouse. The relationship is precious beyond words' description. We thrive in it and because of it. We feel secure in it and can face anything in life, knowing we have it to fall back on when the going gets tough. And it feels so good and satisfying to love and be loved in that way!

But, alas, these relationships are all temporal. They exist for the time being, 'til death do us part. And when death interrupts a relationship like that with its sudden chaotic power to tear away, rip asunder . . . we are left alone, without that love, without that strength, hope, security, and joy our lives and happiness depended upon.

But a one-to-one love-relationship with the Lord, characterized by the vitality and adventure of intimacy, honesty, and trust, is greater than any of these. Its strength is without limitations. Its hope is everlasting and cannot founder. Its security is impregnable. Its joy surpasses all human expectations of the supreme. All this and more: it cannot be taken from us, even by death; it lasts forever.

If you want this kind of authentic, experiential relationship with the One who loves you better and longer than any other person possibly can, then open yourself to receiving it. Give the love you have for the one you've lost to him. You won't lose it; he'll improve it, increase it, and give it back to you. Ask for a growing awareness of the love he already has for you; you'll be amazed at the ways he will do it. Trust him; he'll do his part. Let it happen. Let God love you.

James 4:8

Come near to God and he will come near to you.

Ephesians 3:16–19

I pray that out of his glorious riches he may strengthen you with power through his Spirit in your inner being, so that Christ may dwell in your hearts through faith. And I pray that you, being rooted and established in love, may have the power, together with all the saints, to grasp how wide and long and high and deep is the love of Christ, and to know this love that surpasses knowledge—that you may be filled to the measure of all the fullness of God.

Dear precious Lord, I don't know if my soul can take knowing how much you love me! It's so wonderful to think of how well I've been loved by the one I've lost. And your love for me must be so much greater. Yet I have the need for experiencing more of your love. So give me the faith I need to allow your Spirit to strengthen me and to make me more experientially aware of how wide, how long, how high, and how deep your active, energetic love for me really is. Thank you so much for that love. All glory and praise to the One who loves so perfectly! In your name. Amen.

29

Grieve
with hope

When you were a small child, you probably looked upon yourself and those special people around you as immortal. Perhaps it was not so much a conscious, intellectual understanding, for you saw that other people died. But deep inside, you wanted to believe, insisted upon thinking, that you and those you loved would never die.

This way of thinking was no accident, no total self-delusion. Because there is something inside every one of us that tells us we are meant to always live.

The truth about the matter, however, is that it is our inner self, not our physical presence, that possesses eternal consciousness of its existence. And as we mature in growing up, we come to realize the difference between physical death on the one hand and everlasting spiritual death on the other. We know that the essence of our being will never cease to exist, whether in ongoing living or dying. That's why we choose to accept the grace of God through Jesus Christ who gives us eternal life with him instead of the everlasting, conscious existence of spiritual death away from him.

So there is hope for a Christian to cling to when another Christian dies, a reassurance that the one we love, though he is no longer with us, has not really ceased to exist. He is not here, but in the presence of perfect goodness and love. He is no longer a fellow partaker in suffering, struggling, and living imperfectly, but now experiences the kind of perfect joy you and I can't quite imagine or understand but find peace and comfort in contemplating.

Still, those of us left behind continue to reside in a world of many sufferings, trials, and imperfections. We grieve for our losses, and rightly so. But because we are the children of God, we can grieve with hope. The birth of each new spring means much more to us than the poetic insight into life as being eternal because it continues in cycles. For us it means rebirth of the individual soul and reminds us that, even as we share in Christ's sufferings, we also shall share in the glory and life of his resurrection.

So the next time you see the sun pushing its way through the waning violence of storm clouds, think of the awesome power of God's love overcoming and defeating all the miseries we experience in this life. When you notice the first signs of the eternal spring persisting in its coming forth at the close of a long, hard winter, let it remind you of the dynamic power of the Spirit generating the new birth of the human soul. And when you observe the Holy Day of Easter, let your mind drink in all the assurance, promise, and hope every Christian has in the resurrection of Jesus Christ.

Grieve, yes. But grieve as one who has hope. That wonderful, inexpressible hope in the eternality of life which has been evidenced by Jesus Christ as belonging to each of his own.

John 11:25–26
> Jesus said to her, "I am the resurrection and the life. He who believes in me will live, even though he dies; and whoever lives and believes in me will never die. Do you believe this?"

1 Thessalonians 4:13
> Brothers, we do not want you to be ignorant about those who fall asleep, or to grieve like the rest of men, who have no hope.

*Almighty and glorious God, thank you for the promise of Easter.
O Lord, we'd have no hope without your resurrection! Life would
be meaningless, empty, dull. Thank you that Jesus Christ rose on
the third day and is now at the Father's side acting as our advocate
when the devil accuses us of unrighteousness. Thank you that in
Jesus' death we have been cleansed and our accounts with you
settled; and that in his coming to life again, we have the hope of
eternal life with you after death. And thank you that we can be
comforted by our knowledge of and faith in the cross and the empty
tomb when our fellow-believers go ahead of us to meet you.
Through Jesus Christ. Amen.*

30

Let peace come into your grief

When you lose a Christian friend or relative, letting hope come into your grief is not so difficult because it is part of your faith and his. You can feel assured of where he is right now and that all he is experiencing in his new existence is the best God has to offer. Too, there is hope that you will see him again one day. Even now you may sense that he is with you in spirit. These can be of great comfort to you and encouragement, too, to make of your grief a creative, productive experience.

But what if you aren't sure that you can have that kind of hope for the one you grieve for? What if he made a commitment to Christ before others but lived his life in such a way that you doubt he really experienced God's grace? What if he never got around to publicly confessing the Savior but appeared to be Christ-like in his actions? Suppose he flatly denied the Lord and lived in his own way. What can you do in such a case?

Perhaps there's no greater sorrow than that which comes upon a Christian when his heart and mind are filled with doubts and fears concerning the salvation of a loved one who has died. The thought of a final parting, never to meet again, is heartbreaking. But even more agonizing is the thought of his eternal separation from God. And you may think, "If only I had been a more responsible witness to him," or "If only I hadn't given up on him," or "If only I had been able to reach him in a more effective way for Christ." These thoughts create the deepest feelings of guilt and regret one can bear.

If you are struggling with these thoughts and feelings, surely you'd like for them to be resolved. They are part of the grief work you have before you. Take a look, then, at what you have to deal with, and you can proceed from there.

First of all, are you beset by the "if onlys"? Are your accusations against yourself as a Christian witness valid? If you think they may be so, then go through the steps to erasing your guilt: confessing, seeking God's forgiveness, accepting his forgiveness, and forgiving yourself. As always, the last part is the most difficult. You may have to go through these steps many times before you can complete them with the last one. But do it as often as you have to until you internalize the fact that you can and do forgive yourself.

And second, consider these things. Every person is responsible for himself in his relationship to God; nobody else can meet that responsibility for him. And at the same time, God meets his full responsibility in relation to that person; no individual has need of someone else to move or persuade God to be for him. So, aside from seeking to nurture another's relationship with God and trying to influence it for good, there is absolutely nothing we can do about its outcome. Our duty and privilege as interested bystanders ends with the influence of our witness. We have no right of assuming responsibility for the kind of relationship it turns out to be.

Nor can we always know what exists between another and God. Some people are just too private to tell us. Some wait until the last minute, so to speak, before acknowledging the Savior and have no opportunity to tell us. Whatever the reason, we have to recognize and accept that it's their relationship, not ours, and we may never know for sure how it is between them.

Acknowledge that. Trust the Lord to have done everything he could do to have won that soul. Trust him to be the judge of what's transpired between them. Leave the matter in the hands of the most capable and merciful of fathers, for that's where it belongs now.

And after you've left it there, ask him for the enlightenment he knows you need so that you can have the comfort and peace of mind he wants you to have. Then, accept the peace he will give you, knowing that you do not have to have positive proof of that which gives you peace.

All of this is difficult to do because our love for the other wants to be possessive, protective, and in control of his well-being. It's difficult, but it's possible for you, with the Lord's help. And it works; it helps; it takes care of this burden in a positive, constructive way.

Let go of your desire to know. Trust the one you love into God's hand. Take hold of the peace your heavenly Father is longing to give you. You will be so glad you did.

Romans 11:33–36
> Oh, the depth of the riches of the wisdom and knowl-
> edge of God!
>> How unsearchable his judgments,
>> and his paths beyond tracing out!
> "Who has known the mind of the Lord?
> Or who has been his counselor?"
> "Who has ever given to God,
>> that God should repay him?"
> For from him and through him and to him are all
> things.
>> To him be the glory forever! Amen.

Romans 14:12–13
> So then, each of us will give an account of himself to God. Therefore let us stop passing judgment on one another.

Lord, I praise you and thank you that you are our God and that you have a personal, unique relationship with each one of us. Thank you, too, for giving us relationships one with another so that we may share in your love for us; and that you involve us in your ministry and the spreading of the good news to others. Where I have failed in these things, help me to recognize my true mistakes and seek forgiveness. And where I try to act as judge for you, forgive that, too. Give my mind the peace that understands that you, not I, are in control of all lives and judge each one mercifully and justly. Help me to let you be God and to remember my place and responsibility as your child. In Jesus' name. Amen.

31

Don't quit now

Healing takes time. So does grief work. It is a process of healing just as much as recuperation from disease or the mending of a broken bone.

So, know that working through your grief will require time. Probably more than you'll expect or want. But certainly as much as is necessary.

Perhaps you could be more patient with the passing of time if it weren't for the obstacles that occasionally get in the way. Like the disappointing setbacks that occur at times, which lead you to discover that you haven't healed or grown as much as you'd thought. Like having to deal with the same thing over and over again until you begin to wonder if you'll ever conquer it. Like growing tired of grief work, period.

Those times come. The going gets rough and drawn-out, and you seem to be getting nowhere. So you want to sit down and quit.

But don't quit. Look at the progress you've made. Surely there's something you can count as progress since you began. Think of where you might be if you had done no grief work at all. What would you have done with the feelings if you hadn't grieved constructively? You would have had to do something with them. And think of where you want to go from here, the problems you want to be free of, how you'd like your life to be. Are all those goals worth the work? Sure, they are.

Rest a while, recommit yourself to the task before you, ask the Lord's help one more time, and get on with the living again.

2 Corinthians 4:8–9, 16

> We are hard pressed on every side, but not crushed; perplexed, but not in despair; persecuted, but not abandoned; struck down, but not destroyed. . . . Therefore we do not lose heart. Though outwardly we are wasting away, yet inwardly we are being renewed day by day.

Psalm 31:24

> Be strong and take heart,
>   all you who hope in the LORD.

Oh yes, Lord, it is indeed grief work. I get so thwarted, so disappointed, so sick of it all. Will it never, ever end? Will I never get better? Is becoming whole again a real possibility? Sometimes it doesn't seem so. I want to forget it all and run away. I wish I could change my identity and be another person in another place. I'm just so tired of it all! I'm not able to agree with Paul and say I never feel crushed or despairing or abandoned. He was quite a man of faith, Lord—one that is much stronger than mine. But it wasn't easy for him just because he had the will, the determination, the faith. No, he tells us the secret: his inner self was being renewed by you every day. That's how he was able to rise above his problems. I must ask, then, for the same thing. Let your Holy Spirit revitalize my spirit, soul, and body, dear Lord. I will wait upon you to renew my strength, for my hope is indeed in you. In Jesus' strong and blessed name I pray. Amen.

32

Practice the art of thankful living

There was a song popular years ago which spoke of counting blessings instead of sheep. A fair prescription for worry or insomnia, but a better one for living all of life through the good times and the bad.

The art of living thankfully is contrary to human nature, however. We naturally tend to forget to be thankful when we prosper, and to grumble and despair when we do not. We're inclined to be "spiritual brats" who don't appreciate what our Father gives or does for us, and who complain when something doesn't go our way. All of us do it or have been guilty of it at some time in our lives. It's part of the natural self.

But a maturing Christian will discover, as he reads the Word, that one of our instructions is to be thankful in all things. And when one recognizes this and puts it into practice, he is learning the art of thankful living.

Why are we instructed to live thankfully? Not just because it's only right that we should. It's not merely an arbitrary instruction God made up one day to keep us in our place. All of God's mandates do, of course, remind us of who we are in relation to the One who made us, saves us, and is Lord over us and all we have. But they also serve to benefit us and the quality of our lives. They are for our good in a very practical sense of the word.

When we are thankful for the good things that come our way, we are honoring God instead of ourselves or what we do. We are acknowledging him as the source of "every good and perfect gift." And he in turn honors this kind of recognition from grateful, submissive children by blessing us even more.

When we are thankful in the misfortunes that occur in our lives—even the large and small ordeals we suffer because of grief—we are honoring God again. Not as being the source of evil, for this is not so. But as being *present* in every one of our difficulties, eagerly desiring to bring much good from them if we will only let him.

You see, a truly thankful mind will also be a trusting, obedient one. And when we're that cooperative with the Lord, his power is free to work good out of our circumstances. But a thankless mind will have difficulty being trusting and obedient, and such an attitude will limit the power of the Spirit within to take action in our behalf.

Have you tried the art of thankful living? Or are you responding to God's control over your life like a selfish and spoiled child of the King?

1 Thessalonians 5:16–18

Be joyful always; pray continually; give thanks in all circumstances, for this is God's will for you in Christ Jesus.

Psalm 103:1–5

Praise the LORD, O my soul;
   all my inmost being, praise his holy name.
Praise the LORD, O my soul,
   and forget not all his benefits.
He forgives all my sins
   and heals all my diseases;
he redeems my life from the pit
   and crowns me with love and compassion.
He satisfies my desires with good things,
   so that my youth is renewed like the eagle's.

Dear God, your ways aren't our ways. We deal in reason and rationalizations, but you deal in truth and light. And now I see another secret of your wisdom in instructing us to give thanks. Help me to internalize this truth so that I may come to practice it as naturally as breathing. Only your Holy Spirit can lead my heart into being thankful. Help me to put my reasoning and rationalizing aside and to let him create in me an ever thankful heart. I ask in the name of the Savior. Amen.

33

Come to terms with death

Healing the wound of grief comes easier if you come to terms with death. After all, were it not for death, there would be no loss, no wound, no grief.

It's one thing to philosophize about death or offer solemn Christian platitudes to someone in grief when you haven't suffered a great personal loss yourself. But it's quite another thing to find comfort in those thoughts when it's you who's suffering in the depths of sorrow. So ask yourself how you feel about death now. Your attitude toward it is important to becoming whole again.

Come to terms with death, for it's impossible for you to truthfully deny that one particular act of dying has changed your life. Come to terms with it constructively. The result will be *not* that you become more miserable, but that you will receive a fresher, more mature insight into the precious meaning of life.

Consider these thoughts, for example. It's true that death is an ending, but only in terms of the finishing of a phase of life which then proceeds into another phase. It's easier for the Christian, more than anyone else in the world, to view death not as the final termination of a life, but as the third and final birth. I was born into physical life; I was reborn into spiritual life; I shall be born again into immortality.

When I was in my mother's womb, my environment was totally different from this life's. I had no concept of the size and nature of this world. Before I became a Christian, I was certain only of the world I saw and moved in. I had no understanding of what it meant to live life as a child of God. So it is with the third birth that awaits me—I feel "at home" in this life because I am assisted and nourished by faith, but the concept of eternal life with God in another place is as incomprehensible to me as any other experience which is yet to be explored.

Only the process of nature pushing me out into the world could compel me to leave the warm, comfortable womb for the unknown. Only the working of the Holy Spirit could move me toward the adventure of being born again in Christ and growing in him. Only the inevitable event we call death will cause me to give way to the third birth.

Each of these three life-changes is a dramatic upheaval for human beings. They are often traumatic, too, for each is an extreme rearrangement of life as we have previously known it. They are ventures into the unknown which we perceive as mysterious and therefore frightening.

It is a natural thing, then, that I do not want to die, that I do not want anyone I love to die. Buy my faith tells me this: the death of our bodies will only rearrange our existence, not end it; and while we remain here still, we must do the best we can to encourage one another in fulfilling the purpose of our earthly lives while God's grace allows us the time in which to do it.

1 Corinthians 15:54–55
> When the perishable has been clothed with the imperishable, and the mortal with immortality, then the saying that is written will come true:
>> "Death has been swallowed up in victory."
>> "Where, O death, is your victory?
>> Where, O death, is your sting?"

Revelation 21:4
> "He will wipe every tear from their eyes. There will be no more death or mourning or crying or pain, for the old order of things has passed away."

Lord, being a genuine follower of Christ is the hardest thing in life to do, but oh, how much joy and hope it brings! How well your Spirit helps us to understand life and death and the good and positive meanings you want us to find in them. I fear death, Lord, but I can also accept it in light of my faith in you. To come to terms with death, Father, gives meaning to my life and the lives of others. How I thank you for the victory you give me in understanding the greatest of all victories your Son has already won! In his name. Amen.

34

Let the little ones grieve

Children have feelings, too. They suffer, too, when someone important to them dies. Adults often think, however, that because children are not mature human beings, their feelings aren't important. But such thinking is wrong. And unjust. And harmful to their psyches.

The children in your family deserve the privilege of being free to express their grief. Their right is the same as yours. Their need is the same.

Let a child cry, if he wants to express his sorrow in that way, without shaming him or trying to divert his attention to some other subject. Let him say how sad or angry or guilty or afraid he feels. Listen attentively and answer him, not with your own grief in mind, but with a child's heart and intellectual understanding in mind.

These little sessions hardly ever last very long. Let him express what he wants to as long as he wants to, but do not press him beyond the point he willingly takes himself.

Help him to learn how to express grief positively. It's really very simple and easy to do. To illustrate, suppose you detect anger in something he says about his grandfather's death. Ask him, "Do you feel angry because Grandpa died?" If he replies in the affirmative, then ask, "Do you know why you feel that way?" He will answer as well as he can because he knows now that he has your ear and concern. Then, reaffirm his right to have feelings with, "It's O.K. for you to feel that way. I've felt it, too. But then I got to thinking . . . " and conclude your statement with something rational and positive for him to think about.

A child will feel so much better if you listen to him and guide him in expressing his feelings. Too, he will be learning a valuable lesson about living which adults may have failed to teach you while you were young: how to grieve constructively.

And you can learn from him, too, for when he is properly led, a child lets his grief heal more promptly than most adults do. Try seeing your own grief through the precious faith of a child, and you will see that there is much an adult can learn from one of these little ones.

Matthew 19:14
> Jesus said, "Let the little children come to me, and do not hinder them, for the kingdom of heaven belongs to such as these."

Matthew 18:4
> "Therefore, whoever humbles himself like this child is the greatest in the kingdom of heaven."

I have been much like the disciples, Lord, who wanted the children out of the way. Because I find death and grief so hard to bear, I have feared their questions. They are so straightforward and honest, Lord, not like me at all! Yet they do have feelings of grief, feelings I can't protect or will away. So, help me with the children, dear God, and teach me the simplicity of their love and faith. Heal them, too, just as I have asked you to heal my own broken heart. In the name of Jesus I pray. Amen.

35

Turn on the Light!

You and I are peculiar creatures. We pride ourselves on our intellectual capacities, our knowledge, and our ability to reason things out. But so often our thinking is faulty and not at all logical.

For instance, when a storm comes up in the middle of the day and brings darkness into the rooms of our homes or offices, we say, "The sun isn't shining any more," or "The sun went behind a cloud."

But neither of these is true. The sun is still shining behind that dark and threatening cloud. Ask the pilot of the jet airliner that just landed. He'll tell you so. And the sun hasn't moved from its place; it remains still. Ask the scientist. He'll testify to that. Rather, that which prevents our seeing the sun and obstructs its rays from getting through to us, that which moves here or there creating the condition of darkness, are the storm clouds.

Like the clouds in the sky, many of the negative things in life are easily apparent. Their evidence speaks loudly for themselves. You don't even have to look for them to know they exist.

But, as with the sun behind the clouds, much of what is good and positive in life has to be searched out to be noticed and sometimes appreciated on the power of faith alone.

Logic says the sun is real and the clouds that often cover it are also real. Likewise, the joy and peace of God are real; the despair and depression of grief are real. Both are conditions existing simultaneously. Both require acknowledgement if we are going to think in terms of truth. Therefore, just as we ought to exercise our faith in God and his care for us in times of inner darkness, so must we also consider dealing positively with the negative feelings that hit us like a dark and dreary storm. It only makes sense that we do.

What do you find yourself doing when the rooms of your heart and mind become darkened by depression and despondency? Perhaps your faith is strong enough to acknowledge that God is there, that he hasn't stopped being, that he hasn't gone away. I hope it is, for that is your first step toward victory. But what if knowing that doesn't dispel the darkness? What if knowing he is up there somewhere, blocked out by the darkness but sure to shine upon you again someday, is not enough to help you get through today?

Then is the time to remind yourself that God is not only "out there" but also within you. Just as you remind yourself, when a day grows dark, that you have available some kind of light-resource—such as a lamp, a flashlight, or even a candle— which you can turn on or ignite to give light to your room.

So, when depression makes everything around you dark, frightening, and threatening, turn on the Light! Or, if you think you may have had a "power failure," ignite the candle within you with fuel from the Word or prayer.

It's a waste of time and spiritual and psychic energy to merely sit out the inner storm. And it's a futile and frustrating exercise to try to drive out the darkness on your own power alone. Don't sit in the dark, don't try to will it away. Just turn on the Light of the God of all comfort. And the day's despair will lose its chill, the darkness in your mind will fade away in the increasing glow of the peace and joy that is in Jesus Christ.

John 8:12
> When Jesus spoke again to the people, he said, "I am the light of the world. Whoever follows me will never walk in darkness, but will have the light of life."

Isaiah 26:3
> You will keep in perfect peace
> him whose mind is steadfast,
> because he trusts in you.

O Lord, you know what I do when depression hits. I put aside the peace you give and indulge my soul in the darkness of sorrow and self-pity. I say there's nothing I can do about it. But there really is. Teach me how to turn on the Light within me. Show me the switch and lead me to learn how to activate that energy that will flood the light of peace and comfort into my heart. Help me to know from experience the meaning of that phrase, "the joy of the Lord is my strength." Lead me into the habit of keeping you and all your illuminating power in the center of my life. I ask in Jesus' wonderful name. Amen.

36

Get the most from Christmas

"Christmas won't ever be the same again." You're right. It won't be the same in terms of who is there to share it with you.

But that's the only difference of a negative kind. Christmas is still a time of special joy and wonder. More than the gaiety of parties, more than the delightful anticipation of children, more than the gathering of loved ones to eat a sumptuous feast and exchange gifts, Christmas is special because of what and who it celebrates. The coming of a King, a Savior, the very Son of God in human flesh. That's why we have Christmas. All else are things beside.

Perhaps it's been a long time since you've really celebrated the true joy of Christmas' miracle. Perhaps you've been too busy years before in concentrating on the lesser, earthly things. Perhaps you don't look forward to such celebrating again because it would be too painful to note the absence. That is quite understandable.

If you're dreading your next Christmas, let me offer some suggestions to help you through. Cut down on the number of secular activities if you can. Play it low-key, enjoying the most of what you do participate in. And instead of concentrating on all the secondary things we've put into the holiday, focus the attention of your heart and mind on the cause of all this celebration. Quietly, by yourself or in the fellowship of believers, meditate upon the person of Jesus Christ: who he is, why his Father sent him, what he did for all mankind, and what he is going to do when he comes again. Get into the wonder of Christmas as often as you can in the days preceding December 25th. And on that special day, make your celebration one of adoration and awe, just like the shepherds did so many centuries ago.

You'll not only have a peaceful Christmas, but you'll also have a joyous one, even in the midst of grief.

Isaiah 9:6–7
>   For to us a child is born,
>   to us a son is given,
>   and the government will be on his shoulders.
>   And he will be called
>   Wonderful Counselor, Mighty God,
>   Everlasting Father, Prince of Peace.
>   Of the increase of his government and peace
>   there will be no end.

Colossians 1:15–20
>   He is the image of the invisible God, the firstborn over all creation. For by him all things were created: things in heaven and on earth, visible and invisible, whether thrones or powers or rulers or authorities; all things were created by him and for him. He is before all things, and in him all things hold together. And he is the head of the body, the church; he is the beginning and the firstborn from among the dead, so that in everything he might have the supremacy. For God was pleased to have all his fullness dwell in him, and through him to reconcile to himself all things, whether things on earth or things in heaven, by making peace through his blood, shed on the cross.

How I have dreaded Christmas, Lord. And that shouldn't be so! For without it and what it means, there would be absolutely no hope, no love, no peace of mind. Lead me into your Scriptures, dear God, so that I may meditate upon the greatest event in history: God condescending to become one of us so that he could identify with us and save us. Ease the pain of that notable absence I will know in the midst of my celebrating this event. Restore to me the joy there is in your salvation. And help me to worship you this season in spirit and in truth. In the name above every name I pray. Amen.

37

Get to know yourself

Don't settle for just surviving the blow of loss, or even the healing of your grief. Go further than these—dare to grow.

Grow in self-knowledge. Find out who you are. You are not the same person you were before grief. Your loss has changed your life both outwardly and inwardly.

Don't be afraid to discover yourself. You may not be as great as you think you are, but at the same time, you aren't as "bad" either. Take a realistic look at yourself so that you can discover the potential that needs to be nurtured and developed, as well as the self-defeating mechanisms that need to be discarded or changed.

And love yourself. Not in spite of what you find within, but *because* you are the human being you are, faults and all, and *because* of who you can become with God's help and your cooperation.

Remember that the secret to attaining self-knowledge lies within your willingness to disclose yourself to someone else. It takes courage to do that. It takes a conscious effort to avoid the temptation to deal only in surface conversation about the weather or yesterday's baseball scores, or to talk about others rather than yourself, or to communicate only your intellectual ideas and opinions rather than your innermost thoughts and how they cause you to feel and do the things you do.

Difficult, yes—especially if you've never done it before. And impossible, yes, to ever fully know the person you are. But it is possible to know yourself *better!* And you can live more effectively for yourself and for Jesus Christ when you do.

Just be sure to take care in selecting the person to whom you will reveal yourself. It must be someone you can trust. Someone who loves you as himself. Someone who is not afraid of knowing the real you or even himself.

You see, as you tell another the truth about your secret self, that same secret will be revealed to you. You will begin to get in touch with the person inside you and learn to love and accept him, even if he is not perfect. Furthermore, you'll find that the adventure of such an encounter with another opens up new horizons of self-understanding that just can't be had with all the private introspection in the world.

And there's even more. This kind of sharing fosters self-growth. Little by little, you'll begin to discover the particular worth within yourself that you can capitalize upon . . . the games you play that you don't really need and can be rid of . . . the self-defeating habits and ways of thinking you can change into assets. And one day you'll realize that you are making some changes in your life for the better. And what does change mean? It means you're growing, evolving, maturing into the person Christ knows you can become and wants you to become for his glory and his service.

So, you see, getting to know the person you are and who you can become—both because of your loss—is not only something valuable and positive you can do for your own well-being. It's also the means to spiritual growth, a way of honoring God, and a key to unlocking the door to that new, re-directed life he has planned for you.

Dare to take the risk of coming to understand yourself better, and take it under the leadership of the Spirit who lives within you. You've nothing to lose but self-delusion, false pride, and the hangups that prevent you from living a more abundant life in Jesus Christ.

Psalm 139:1–2
> O Lord, you have searched me
>> and you know me.
> You know when I sit and when I rise;
>> you perceive my thoughts from afar.

Ecclesiastes 4:9–10
> Two are better than one,
>> because they have a good return for their work:
> If one falls down,
>> his friend can help him up.
> But pity the man who falls
>> and has no one to help him up!

Dear Father, empower me with your Spirit to take the risk of knowing myself better. You know who I am much better than I'll ever know me, so lead and guide me in self-discovery with another. I don't know exactly how that works in a friendship, and frankly, I'm afraid of it. But I do know I can trust you, and I do know that a friendship founded in you and developed by you is the safest and most joyful kind. So, lead me to that person, help both of us to keep our relationship centered in you, and teach both of us what you'd have us know about ourselves and about you. In Jesus' name and for his glory. Amen.

38

Grow
in love

There's another way in which you can grow from your grief. You can grow in your understanding and experience of the real meaning of love. Dare to grow in love. It's the most precious blessing you can receive from your ordeal of pain and suffering, for out of it you can come to know the love of God in a way you never dreamed possible before.

You can never grow enough in love, because love will never pass away. That must mean it has no limits, no bounds, no one point at which you can say you've "arrived" and know all there is to know of it. Indeed, if God is love, and he is, then love is God. It naturally follows, then, that there's always room to grow where love is concerned.

And what an adventure of growing! Just think of it. There is more for you to learn about how much God loves you. More to learn about your own love for him and how the Spirit within you can increase it. More to learn about the deeper meaning of the words to that old hymn, "Blest be the tie that binds our hearts in Christian love." There's a lot to learn! And thank God, we will never "graduate" from this school but continue it in heaven and for all eternity.

But why wait until you get to heaven? Why not make it your goal to grow more in love while you're still here and have so great a need for it?

Ask him for this kind of growth. He'll surely teach you, for he wants you to have it. But, as with everything else in the Christian life, you have to do your part, too, in cooperation with him. Desire a greater knowledge and experience of love. Expect him to give it and continue to teach you for the rest of your life. Wait patiently for the times he will choose in his wisdom to teach you. And obey every instruction of the Spirit, for growing in love is something that comes best by practicing it.

1 John 4:16

> And so we know and rely on the love God has for us. God is love. Whoever lives in love lives in God, and God in him.

John 13:35

> "All men will know that you are my disciples if you love one another."

Kind and loving Father, I do want to grow in love. I want to experience the depths of its joys in every possible way you have in mind for me. I see you as the God of love; I've known you to love me in so many ways and so well. Teach me more, Lord! And help me to respond to your instruction with a submissive will and a hopeful, expectant spirit. These things I ask in the name of the Lord of Love. Amen.

39

Follow
the new road

Be brave enough to grow outwardly, too. Take stock of what you've done with your life thus far. Are any changes in what you do with your time in order? Or attractive to you? It could be God is leading you toward doing something which was not possible or probable before your loss. It could be this "something" is part of the good he wants to bring out of your tragic circumstances. Like developing a talent or gift you weren't aware you had, or a revival of interest in one you've had all along but haven't used in a good while, if at all. Like going back to school, whether it be college or a special kind of training. Like changing your present career to another you feel more suited for. Like getting involved in community resources that exist to help people in need.

Or it could be this "something" does not involve a change in what you do but how you do it. If you feel no leadership to do something new, take stock of how you have performed in life. Is there anything positive you can take from your grief experience and implement into your job, or your family affairs, or your church? Has the Lord given you something in grief which you can use to serve him elsewhere? Like taking his power and love with you to work, or improving communication with your family members, or being bold enough to stand before a group of people for the first time and say, "This is what God has done for me in my sorrow." And how about this: helping another person new to grief who is just as lost in it as you were at the beginning.

All things work together for good to those who love God

and are called according to his purpose, yes. But it's not just for your good alone that he does this, though he's more than gracious to make it so. It's also for the good of his Kingdom and for his glory, but only if we take what he gives us and put it to work in our outward lives so that the Kingdom may continue to thrive and his glory and grace be revealed to others through the example of our lives.

So, grow toward that re-directed life he's laying out for you. You'll see the signposts along the way if you'll only continue to look for them. He'll lead you to what he wants you to do, just as he leads you through the valley of the shadow—one step at a time. And you don't have to worry about succeeding or failing—that's his job. Yours is to be willing and to step out on faith at his direction.

Psalm 143:10
> Teach me to do your will,
>> for you are my God;
> may your good Spirit
>> lead me on level ground.

John 15:5
> "I am the vine; you are the branches. If a man remains in me and I in him, he will bear much fruit; apart from me you can do nothing."

Lord, you've been so gracious to me. And I expect there is even more in your storehouse of blessings designated to be mine if I'll allow you to do the good pleasure of your will within my life. I believe that you have more good in mind for me to receive than I can possibly imagine! Just help me, Lord, to trust you and obey you and to rely on you at all times for my strength. I only need to know direction for one step at a time. Give it, Lord, and I will take it and trust the rest of the way to you. Thank you for giving me the privilege of being your servant as well as your child and your friend. Thank you for setting me on a new road that will add to the meaning of my life. In Christ's name and for his sake. Amen.

40

Become whole again

I remind you again that all processes require time in which to accomplish them. And most processes of growth are likely to have their ups and downs. Both of these will be characteristic of your grief work. Don't let them defeat you. You are already on your way! Become whole again.

When you encounter a setback in grief, you may think of it as failure. It isn't, just as a great stride forward doesn't mean instant success. Understand and accept that you may experience both in your grief work. Look upon them as signs that things are progressing as they normally do.

Just be sure that as regards both up and down situations, you take from them something valuable you have learned. Treat the ups for what they are: positive times to enjoy and grow on, not necessarily signals that grief work is over. And turn the downs into something positive by making them stepping stones for growth, else they'll become hindrances and irritants, like rocks in your shoes.

Ask yourself now and then, "What am I learning?" and "How am I changing?" Learning and changing signify growth, and if you're growing, you're also healing. Both of them are part of becoming whole again.

Occasionally it will do you good to evaluate the progress you've made as well as what yet remains to be worked on. Since only you have known the depths of your pain, only you can know the full value of progress you've made. So take a look backward every so often to see where you have been (a daily journal helps here), and you will be encouraged in a way no other's words can inspire.

Finally, take courage in remembering that your grief work will not go on forever. It really is a process with an attainable end. And one day you may discover that you've begun to think of your loss as a transition point in your life. It was a traumatic, tragic, sorrowful event, most certainly, but one which you, with the help of God, are turning into something positive and valuable for yourself and for others. Then you will know that you are really making it. Soon you will be able to pronounce yourself whole again.

Psalm 40:1–3
> I waited patiently for the LORD;
>   he turned to me and heard my cry.
> He lifted me out of the slimy pit,
>   out of the mud and mire;
> he set my feet on a rock
>   and gave me a firm place to stand.
> He put a new song in my mouth,
>   a hymn of praise to our God.
> Many will see and fear
>   and put their trust in the LORD.

Romans 15:13
> May the God of hope fill you with all joy and peace as you trust in him, so that you may overflow with hope by the power of the Holy Spirit.

My Lord and my God, you have been so good and merciful to me. You have preserved my life and begun to make it whole again. When I think of the sufferings and trials of my grief, I cannot praise you enough for bringing me to where I am today. You have dealt bountifully with me. You have sheltered me, upheld me, and set me on my two feet again so that I may walk in life anew. You've given me strength, comfort, hope, love, and even joy in the midst of my pain. There is none to compare with you, dear Lord! I see the light, faintly shining at the end of the long, dark tunnel. Continue to be my guide and keep my feet from slipping. Direct my ways for all my life. And I will honor you and all you have done in me for the rest of my days. In my blessed Savior's name. Amen.

suggestions for further reading

On Death and Grief

Bayly, Joseph. *The View from a Hearse: A Christian View of Death.* David C. Cook, Elgin, Illinois. Takes a hard look at the facts about death and our attitudes toward it. Helpful toward developing a healthy, realistic view of the subject in light of the Christian faith.

Grollman, Earl A., editor. *Concerning Death: A Practical Guide for the Living.* Beacon Press, Boston. A guide to dealing constructively with the fact of death and the feelings of grief. Includes the topics of children and death, the widow and widower, and cultural attitudes toward death.

Hough, Robert Ervin. *The Christian After Death.* Moody Press, Chicago. Offers scripturally based answers to questions concerning death, the resurrection, and life after death. Author is a Presbyterian minister.

Jackson, Edgar N. *When Someone Dies.* Fortress Press, Philadelphia. A short but concise book on the subjects of death, grief, and children's grief. Excellent for the person who has never before been acquainted with deep grief.

Moody, D. L. *Heaven.* Moody Press, Chicago. Discusses all we ever wonder about heaven and its inhabitants. Based on Scripture. Communicates joy and hope.

Westburg, Granger E. *Good Grief.* Fortress Press, Philadelphia. An excellent little book emphasizing the need to grieve constructively. Author is a Lutheran clergyman who writes out of his belief that many instances of physical illness are results of grief which has not been constructively expressed.

Personal Experiences

Claypool, John. *Tracks of a Fellow Struggler.* Word Books, Waco, Texas. Written by a Southern Baptist minister whose young daughter died of leukemia. An account of his grief, including anger, despair, and resignation. A powerful testimony to God's grace in strengthening one's faith through the experience of loss.

Huffman, Carolyn. *Bloom Where You Are*. Vision House, Santa Ana, California. An account of this woman's grief for the death of her small son. Shows the power of God to bring joy and purpose out of tragedy.

Marshall, Catherine. *Beyond Our Selves*. McGraw-Hill, New York. Relates the author's growth toward meaning and joy after the death of her husband, Peter Marshall. Inspirational and encouraging to those whose lives are left in shambles by a personal loss.

Marshall, Catherine. *Something More*. McGraw-Hill, New York. Written thirteen years after *Beyond Our Selves*. A re-examining of her faith, brought on by new trials and doubts. Told with refreshing honesty and insight into living the Christian life abundantly.

Helping Yourself

Ball, Robert R. *The "I Feel" Formula*. Word Books, Waco, Texas. A primer in self-acceptance and the acceptance of others. Theme of communication and self-knowledge. Excellent for understanding how what we tell ourselves and others affects our relationships. Author is a Presbyterian minister.

Hauck, Paul A. *Overcoming Depression*. Westminster Press, Philadelphia. Treats the subject of depression as resulting from guilt, self-pity, and "other-pity." Also offers a guide to developing the habit of rational thinking. Easy to read.

Mallory, James D., M.D. *The Kink and I*. Victor Books, Wheaton, Illinois. Subtitled "A Psychiatrist's Guide to Untwisted Living." Helps the reader identify and correct the "kinks" that prevent him from becoming the person God intends him to be. Written in the popular style, easy to understand.

Maultsby, Maxie C. *Help Yourself to Happiness*. Institute for Rational Living, New York. Offers a guide for the individual layperson to rational self-counseling. Includes practical illustrations and review questions at the end of each chapter. For the person who is really serious in learning about the subject through application of what he reads. Written by a psychiatrist.

Ogilvie, Lloyd John. *Let God Love You*. Word Books, Waco, Texas. Written by a prominent Presbyterian minister. A well-written series of devotionals taken from the letter Paul wrote to the Philippians. Well worth the reading.

Powell, John, S.J. *Why Am I Afraid to Love?* Argus Communications, Niles, Illinois. Helps the reader understand and face the fear of really loving another. Written in a style that is easy to understand; excellent in insight.

Powell, John, S.J. *Why Am I Afraid to Tell you Who I Am?* Argus Communications, Niles, Illinois. A wonderful little book on the subjects of self-awareness, personal growth, and interpersonal communication. For the person who wants to get to know himself through self-disclosure to another. Enjoyable reading. Enlightening.